Curiosity
Recaptured

Curiosity Recaptured

*Exploring Ways We
Think and Move*

Edited by Jerry Sontag

With a Foreword by Robertson Davies

Mornum Time Press

Published in the United States of America by MORNUM TIME PRESS.
MORNUM TIME PRESS has secured the rights to use all essays
and illustrations in this book.

Book cover and interior design by Marianne Ackerman
209 Mississippi Street, San Francisco, California 94107

Illustrations and cover artwork by Ginger Tate Beringer
1514 Grant Street, Berkeley, California 94703

Library of Congress Catalog Card Number: 96-076522
ISBN 0-9644352-2-5
Printed and bound in the United States of America

Contents

Foreword

THE ALEXANDER TECHNIQUE was known to me for several years before I had direct experience of it. I was impressed by Bernard Shaw's warm words about it in the Preface to *Music in London 1888-89* and by Aldous Huxley's more extended appreciation in *Ends and Means*; indeed I went to a good deal of trouble to get copies of Alexander's books *The Universal Constant in Living* and *Man's Supreme Inheritance*, and could make nothing of them. Alexander was no writer and as I had been convinced from school days that "what is clearly understood may be clearly expressed" I decided that his discovery must remain a mystery to me.

In 1955, however, I began to have serious trouble with my left leg, which lost feeling easily when I was sitting; for a man whose work included a great deal of reviewing concerts and plays, that was serious. Sometimes when I rose at the end of an act I could hardly walk, and was likely to fall. The medical profession, as I experienced it, was unhelpful; doctors drew designs on my leg in yellow chalk, probed it with pins, and told me what I already knew, which was that it was wanting in feeling. They suggested that I might have my back opened, in search of a slipped disc—an ailment very popular at the time. I knew two or three people who had undergone such operations and were worse off than they had been before, so I fled the clinic as fast as I could.

In November of that year I had the good fortune to meet a friend of a friend who was an Alexander enthusiast, and put me in touch with a New York teacher (for there were none at that time in Canada) who was a Miss Lulie Westfeldt, and my wife and I met Miss Westfeldt in January of the following year. She undertook to instruct both of us—for my wife was a keen enthusiast for forms of education which preserved health—and we took daily lessons for a week, by the end of which time Miss Westfeldt had brought my leg into a better frame of mind, and we were both converts to the Technique. From that time forward we visited Miss Westfeldt twice a year for a week's refresher, and in the periods in between we worked on ourselves, and according to her careful and explicit directions. This continued until her death in 1965.

Lulie Westfeldt was a remarkable and delightful person and we three became fast friends. She was "a lady" by the strict definition of the New Orleans of her birth, and her standards of personal behaviour and honour were immovable, but did not in any way inhibit her keen enjoyment of life and her sense of humour. She had suffered polio at the age of seven, and had undergone an operation when she was thirteen that immobilized her right ankle, so that during the years between 1909 and 1929 she was confined to a wheel chair, and was deeply unhappy. But in 1929, on the advice of a friend, she went to London to see Alexander, and after six months of lessons he had her walking again; she joined his first Training Course in 1931 and after four years was a qualified teacher, and herself moved freely, except for what the Irish might call "a slight delay" in her left leg. She rode a horse, she danced, she delighted in the elegant shoes she was now able to wear. Her friendship was very dear to us, and under her guidance we both became convinced Alexandrians.

For me, the educative side of the work was fully as rewarding as the physical improvement. I learned that not everything which is clearly understood may be clearly expressed—not, that is to say, in words, which was the element in which I worked. There are many important things that must be learned from personal experience and frequently from a teacher. I have had several Alexander teachers and I have never had one yet who could explain the work adequately, and the explanations of professional explainers, like Aldous Huxley, are merely confusing; the alignment of head, neck and back must be felt and I doubt if any two people feel it quite alike, because—to quote another dictum drilled into me as a boy—"that which is perceived is perceived in the mode of the perceiver." Our bodies are individual and our sense of our bodies is our own; my wife, the tennis player, does not experience the Alexander work precisely as do I, the sedentary worker. The bad teacher—and I had brief experience of one who was a power-seeker—does not know the work as does the religious fanatic—and I had one of those—or the philosopher who has fled from the world of finance.

Miss Westfeldt was very interesting on this point. Alexander, she said, was unwilling to be drawn into discussion of the psychological aspect of his discovery. This is not astonishing, considering the circumstances of his early life and that he offered his discovery to a pre-Freudian world, where talk of psychology aroused resistance. He did, however, say a few things which Miss Westfeldt treasured, such as, "This work doesn't change you radically; it just makes you more completely and efficiently yourself; if you're a burglar, it will simply make you a better burglar." She likened the work to a form of psycho-analysis, working through the body instead of through the mind, and certainly the releases and flashes of self-recognition give weight to this concept. It is one of the mysteries of psycho-analysis that neither Freud nor Jung seems to have suggested that bodily experience and bodily "use" might have an influence on the psyche. One wonders what combined work upon both might bring about.

As a teacher, Miss Westfeldt was a classicist; the words of Alexander were her gospel, and every lesson was accompanied by ceaseless repetition of the mantra "Neck free; head thought forward to go up; back lengthening, to widen, to drop back." Subsequent teachers have assured me that this is not wholly necessary, but I find it an invaluable reminder. Like Alexander, she worked with the pupil seated, and standing before a mirror, but she deviated from the Master in working also with the pupil lying on a table; she said that Alexander's pupils had the greatest difficulty in persuading him that this was a valid technique, and that they had themselves devised it: Alexander did not adopt it. She described him as a very great teacher, an authoritarian who inspired complete trust. In her early days of instruction she said that she sometimes was overcome with fear and would cry, "I'm going to fall down, F.M.!", to which he would reply imperturbably, "Fall down then, but be sure you fall with the head going up." But she did not fall down, and she described the miracle of the first day on which she was able to take a step. It was a step backward.

As a teacher, she described Alexander as superb, patient and illuminating and demonstrating everything in action rather than in words. She agreed with me that he had small gift for words, but she added that she felt that he did not truly want to explain his Technique, partly for fear of misunderstanding among those who had not undergone training, and partly that deep-rooted reluctance which many innovators feel about imparting their secret to others.

The Technique has played an important part in my life, not only as a guide to physical management and health, but because I am by temperament disposed to examine and probe its psychological aspects. What Alexander called "inhibition," abandonment of bodily effort and conscious management which some other techniques call "non-doing," has helped me through many a difficult situation. A writer is tempted to do his work by wholly inappropriate physical means: he may sit in a contorted posture, his neck awry, his legs wrapped around each other, and his face a mask of tension; or he may slump in despair, when the work will not go forward. There are many ways in which he may yield to what Alexander called "end-gaining"; he sees the end, however dimly and imperfectly, and he struggles toward it, instead of considering the means by which it may be attained. End-gaining, I think, must be one of the things that brings about the condition called Writer's Block.

I do not for an instant suggest that experience of the Technique will make a writer of someone who was not a writer before; but, as Alexander said, if he is a writer, it may well make him a better writer, or at least a writer whose work is less stressful in a notoriously stress-prone profession.

But Oh, the life is short, the art is long! Commitment to the Technique is a lifelong sentence; new aspects of it are continually presenting themselves; new understandings break in after years of concealment; neglect brings sudden revenges. But it keeps the body alive, at ages when many people have resigned themselves to irreversible decline. It keeps the mind alive, for it demands unceasing vigilance.

With all its demands it is worth every moment it asks for, and those once committed to it may well find that they cannot do without it. It is an enlargement of whatever life may be yours.

—*Robertson Davies*

Acknowledgments

THIS PROJECT GREW into a book through the encouragement of many people, and was made possible thanks to the positive reception of Walter Carrington's *Thinking Aloud*—the first title published by Mornum Time Press.

Without the help and skills of the following people, *Curiosity Recaptured* would not exist: Marianne Ackerman's wonderful design and production help; illustrator Ginger Tate Beringer's willingness to trust in her imagination; Robertson Davies's generosity in contributing to this book; Lorelei Sontag's careful editing and unflagging support; and all of the essayists who put their thoughts to paper.

For help with my introduction, special thanks to Linda Avak, Anne Bluethenthal, Joan and Lincoln Diamant, Peter Mangione, Lorelei Sontag, Doug Wiebe, and Andrew Wright. The introduction became richer and clearer thanks to their suggestions.

Finally, I'd like to thank Kathleen Ballard, Sheldon Berkowitz, Sean Carey, Babette Lightner, John Nicholls, Daniel Pevsner, James Saliba, Lois and Richard Sontag, and Samuel Sontag.

Introduction

EACH ESSAY IN THIS BOOK tells a story. Some are about learning a new skill or the excitement of solving a particularly intractable problem. Others reexamine commonplace moments of our days that often go unnoticed. Each writer tells a personal story that takes us from a specific activity being described—whether it is learning to sing or moving away from home—to the impact the activity has on our overall interest and curiosity in daily life. In all these essays, the authors are never far from their subjects, because these are stories of self-discovery.

These self-discoveries are based on the work of F.M. Alexander, who was trying to solve within himself what he thought of as a physical problem. Through self-observation, he recognized a harmful tension pattern. It involved tightening the musculature of the neck, pulling the head back, and interfering with the tone of the back musculature. Alexander found that this pattern of tension was not limited to himself, but was surprisingly widespread.

The Alexander Technique, which developed from these observations, helps uncover the ways specific tension patterns affect our balance, our breathing, and our ability to know accurately where we are in space (our proprioceptive sense). These tension patterns also affect what we think of as our "mental" faculties: our ability to make a decision and then follow through on it, our level of confidence in learning something new, and our overall awareness of our environment.

When tension blocks out information and sensations that are essential for maintaining a sense of novelty in the simplest activities, our field of awareness is reduced. This reduction of awareness dampens our curiosity about the world around us, and makes all forms of learning more difficult. It also leads to chronic physical problems. Each essay in this book addresses the need for the fullest awareness of oneself and one's environment. This focus should come as no surprise, since these essays are written by teachers of the Alexander Technique, and the Technique itself is based on observing oneself in daily life.

Care has been taken to make these essays accessible to the Alexander teacher or student, as well as to the reader unfamiliar with the Technique. Yet, in any field, a specific terminology develops, and the Alexander Technique is no exception. Throughout the essays, such terms as *directions, inhibition, use, primary control*, and *freeing the neck* are used. The *whispered ah*, a method used to help free up breathing and reduce the influence of habits over speech, comes up again and again as the means one writer or another uses to help with a problem. The meanings of these terms are made clear within the context of the essay. In addition, though the authors were not writing collaboratively, each essay sheds light on others in the collection. The result is a practical overview of some of the applications of the Technique in daily life. A bibliography is included to direct the reader to a variety of books which provide further information about the concepts and history of the Technique.

All the essays examine ways to solve problems; two of the essays explore these subjects directly. In "The Chair is Where the Body Meets the Environment," Galen Cranz looks at the challenges of designing chairs, the compromises made by their designers, and the implications of designing and building chairs based on a better understanding of the way the body actually works. In Edward Avak's "Parallel Lives," mathematics, physics, and the Alexander Technique all come together as he takes a look at the ways we problem-solve, and the similarities between two problem-solvers, one a famous mathematician, George Polya, and the other the founder of the Alexander Technique, F.M. Alexander.

The performing arts have long played an important part in the development of the Alexander Technique. Four essays explore the relationship of the Technique to the performing arts. In "Before You Leap," Anne Bluethenthal looks at some of the hazards of conventional dance training, and presents an alternative vision. Greater technical skill and deeper emotional expressiveness are still the goals, but they are achieved with less conflict and effort. In "Born to Sing," Ron Murdock, who combines a practical understanding of the anatomical workings of the voice with an impassioned argument for the role of beauty in singing, takes us on a detailed journey through the world of the voice. From Alex Murray's earliest childhood fingerings on a penny whistle to becoming first flute with the London Symphony, Murray traces his own development as a musician. In "Grabbing the Bird by the Tale," he recounts the pitfalls that he has encountered along the way, and his rediscovery of the joys of playing an instrument. Phyllis Richmond has been involved with theater for the past 20 years. In "The Actor's Consciousness and the Character's Consciousness," she shares with us the skills an actor must develop to convey the playwright's meaning effectively without jeopardizing his or her own health in the process.

Almost everyone engages in some form of physical exercise. The three essays dealing with exercise and sport examine the unconscious habits that interfere with these activities. In "A Two Wheel Essay," Barry Collins takes us on a ride through the streets of London and the back country of France. He looks at the ways thinking affects the cyclist's ability to ride safely, intelligently, and efficiently. Walton White travels through a different landscape—the beaches and hills of Santa Monica, California—on his own two feet. In "Together We Walk," White takes a look at something we have all been doing since our first years of life, and shows us how to experience walking in a wholly new way. Sometimes by becoming a beginner again a deeper understanding of one's own area of expertise emerges. Barbara Kent, a teacher of the Alexander Technique and a professional singer, goes back to basics when she learns how to play tennis in "Love-40." Her insights into studying a skill, or teaching it, are as applicable to swinging a tennis racket as to singing an aria.

In the field of health, Deborah Caplan, a physical therapist and Alexander teacher, takes us on a personal journey from her childhood through defining her own professional identity. "Floating Thoughts" captures what is lost when one gets cut off from a part of oneself. And in "The Alexander Technique in Childbirth," Ilana Machover shares her experiences working with pregnant women, explores her ideas about pain in childbirth, and critiques some of the present models for birth in Europe and the U.S.

Most of us like to control our lives and our destinies. As is demonstrated in very different ways by two of the essays, that is not always possible. In "Meeting the Unexpected," Mary Holland takes us on her travels across borders and professions. When facing the twists and turns of her life, she learns how anticipation and preconceptions about the future color her experiences. In "Grief," Vivien Schapera shares her personal and professional experiences of emotions associated with death and dying. She looks at the ways the Technique helped her and others in processing powerful emotions unleashed by the death of a loved one.

The final essay in the book is by Walter Carrington, a teacher trained by F.M. Alexander in 1936. In "Beyond Words," he looks back sixty years to his first experience reading F.M. Alexander's books, and gives the reader a taste of the challenge of explaining the Technique in words.

Reading through these essays, you will see that the Technique can be applied in as many different ways as there are people to apply it. Although no one wrote an essay on helping a child go to sleep, they could have, as I discovered a few years ago. I was trying to get my two year old son to sleep. At the time, he most enjoyed falling asleep while being held and rocked. So, I was holding him in my arms, while rocking back and forth. He was not going to sleep.

Sleep had never been one of his strong suits, and I was especially irritated that night. I didn't want to be rocking back and forth in this chair. I had things to do.

After a while, I calmed down enough to realize that my neck was tightening, and that I wasn't breathing freely. I became more aware of what I was actually doing, and thought I would at least let myself breathe. Then I realized that the arm and wrist holding my son were unnecessarily tense. I let my wrist free up. I felt a bit better, a little less irritated. Some pleasure at actually holding my child returned. Within a minute my son was asleep.

I had to laugh, not because I had made my son go to sleep—he wouldn't have gone to sleep if he wasn't ready—but because I had actually been keeping him awake!

Whether you play tennis, study mathematics, sit in chairs all day, or just have a child who won't go to sleep at night, these essays may help you rekindle an interest in, and a curiosity about, the way you move through your daily life.

—*Jerry Sontag*

The Chair is Where the Body Meets the Environment

❧ *by Galen Cranz*

But what about your life as a professor?" my friends asked. I never doubted I would continue teaching architecture at U.C. Berkeley, but two friends were listening to me consider spending four years pursuing a second profession as an Alexander Technique teacher. This idea did not appear to be a particularly good career move since my teaching position and my interest in the Alexander Technique seemed to spring from two different sources.

I had gone to graduate school in sociology, specializing in a field of my own definition—the social use of space—and had aspirations to apply this specialty to help architects understand the people for whom they build. My dream of being able to teach in a school of architecture came true, and my research area, broadly speaking, has to do with how people use buildings and space.

But a second dream had emerged from dealing with severe rotatory scoliosis which I have had since I was a 12 years old girl. This condition is called "idiopathic" since the cause is unknown, and accordingly, prescribed treatments had a hit or miss quality. I had started Alexander lessons in my early thirties and found more relief and hope in this self-monitoring system of posture and movement than in more standard osteopathic, chiropractic or allopathic treatments.

A person with a curve as severe as mine was (80 degrees) can expect only a dour future. The standard medical rule of thumb is that for every year of your life the curve worsens by a degree. I could expect to be doubled over sideways, most likely with impaired lung or heart function, and possibly wheel-chair bound by middle or old age. In light of this prospect, my commitment to continuing the progress experienced with the Technique was as strong as my career commitment. Probably the career commitment required the health commitment.

Over and above necessity, however, a dream of service also kept me committed to the Alexander Technique. Since adolescence

I promised myself that if I ever found a way to master this condition I would owe it to others to share what I discovered. I had started to study the Alexander Technique in 1978, but it was the dramatic changes I experienced during a fifth year of lessons with a new teacher in New York that made me realize that I could do more than simply manage my pain; I could actually begin to reform my structure and straighten my spine. And if I could, that meant others could too. Therefore, training to become an Alexander teacher made personal and ethical sense. But academically?

Suddenly, in 1983, while drinking coffee with friends at a French bakery in Oakland, my two dreams came together! I realized I could combine my interests in the body and the environment by studying the part of the environment that we touch with our bodies—chairs. The logic was something like this: the body and the environment touch in three major ways—tools, clothing, and furniture. Obviously, furniture was closer to an architectural scale than the others, and knowing that I would need to narrow the topic even further, I decided to focus on the chair, something everyone has to deal with in daily life, and an object of intense interest to architects who often try their hand at designing them.

Convinced that the Alexander Technique and research into the social use of space might have some things in common, I started Alexander teacher training that same year. I juggled my academic work and my Alexander training over two years until 1986 when I was hospitalized for problems related to my back condition. I took a medical leave from Berkeley in 1987 and started training again in New York City, eventually completing my training in 1990.

Since 1989 I have offered a graduate seminar at the University called "Designing for the Near-Environment" in which I integrate body and design, and which students appreciate deeply. So I knew from experience that I could interest designers in the body and how it meets the environment, but what could I do for Alexander teachers? Does design matter to those interested in the way they use themselves? Specifically, what do people versed in the Alexander Technique care about chairs? After all, an Alexander teacher is, in effect, asking students to ignore the problems posed by the environment. We help people identify and inhibit their habitual response of collapsing onto a chair. We teach people how to avoid slumping in general, but we spend a disproportionate amount of time practicing the simple act of sitting down and standing up from a chair because this action is so common. We seek to transform precisely such everyday habits—not just special exercises or poses. Alexander teachers have been socialized to think that through "good use" people can transcend any strains imposed by the environment. F.M. Alexander himself said that attempting to restore schoolchildren's health through physical design was wrong-headed. He rejected the idea of improving school desks, tables and chairs, stating in his first book that we should not "educate our school furniture, but...educate our children."

Designers, in contrast, are used to the idea of the "environmental fix." Unfortunately, they often forget the human part of the equation and focus all their attention on the physical aspects of chair design. Designers usually do not think it is their responsibility to educate people about how the environment can and should be used. And, indeed, this bias has some merit because no matter how body-conscious one becomes, overcoming the effect of a poorly organized environment is not easy. In my own case, the more conscious and physically sensitive I became, the less I was able to overcome the effects of bad chairs. The more aware I became of the importance of taking responsibility for one's own use, the more irate I became at the negative effects of uncomfortable seats in airplanes, cars, movie theaters, restaurants, lecture halls and auditoriums, and even the soft yielding couches in people's homes.

But whether we are conscious of its effects or not, the environment does shape culture, our bodies, our behavior and our whole selves. Shoes, for example, are a part of the environment that affect us intimately. Both men's and women's feet in the

U.S. mainland are different from the feet of those Hawaiians who have walked the beaches barefoot as children. Compared to theirs our feet look like the victims of moderate Chinese foot binding! Our little toes in particular suffer, and with women the problems multiply: bunions, distorted gait, swayback. Thus, shoes directly shape our bodies and our physical behavior, and moreover they indirectly shape our social behavior and cultural practices. High heels change women's gait directly, and determine indirectly how far they want to walk, how vulnerable they feel and, extrapolating further, how courageous and competent they feel.

At other scales the environment is equally influential. The layout of driveways or corridors determines who becomes friends with whom, at least in socially homogeneous settings like suburbs and dormitories. The environment also functions as a mnemonic, telling us what to do (sit, stand, walk, dance, pray), where (front, side, on or off the carpet), when (morning, everyday, rarely), and how (exuberantly, seriously, routinely), and all this without being told. Altogether the environment is an important medium through which culture is expressed, and part of its power stems from the fact that it works continuously and often without our conscious awareness. Its messages are all the more powerful for being subliminal.

Because they recognize that environmental forces affect us, professional designers deliberately seek to manipulate and control them. Design is a practical art, because it combines structure, social usefulness, and visual pleasure. I think of design as an integrative cultural practice.

But even though a designer attempts to integrate everything, a designed object never can fully solve all problems simultaneously. Designers try to solve more than one problem at a time and formally integrate all those solutions into one seamless whole. Invariably total integration fails because of the competing demands made by science, social practice and art. People who study design as a mental process define design as a wicked problem—that is, one that never has and never can have a single solution.

The form that an object takes has been attributed to "function" and so design is often defined as functional (as opposed to formal and artistic). However, many different forms can come out of similar functions, so form does not automatically follow function. Just as often, the form of a designed object follows failure, not function. That is, someone creates an object that solves several problems simultaneously, but because design is a wicked problem there is always something that is not completely resolved. In addition, social usage changes and evolves, or new materials don't work well with old ones. For these reasons an inventor or designer focuses on the failure and corrects it and adjusts the form of the object accordingly.

Turning to chairs, they are part of this world of practical art. That is, in chairs designers seek to unite social purpose and good looks with safe and economical construction. Integration of these three is the goal but the chair is definitely a wicked problem, meaning that of its three goals some are better resolved than others. It has loose ends, which provide the impetus for further innovation and invention. Chairs have been transformed, elaborated, decorated and manufactured in many ways. In fact, one can characterize decades and centuries by their chairs. This is not because the human body has changed much over the ages, but because designers and the cultures they represent appreciate and neglect different aspects of the body at different periods in history.

If chair design is already a wicked problem, will the application of principles from the Alexander Technique make it pricklier still? I believe that the insights of the Technique have made chair design both impossible and coherent. Let me explain the paradox in the balance of this essay.

The first insight stemming from the Alexander Technique is that a chair should not disturb the capacity of the person to organize and maintain the proper dynamic between the head and neck. The head/neck relationship is not in any way fixed—to the contrary—and accordingly, the chair should not, by its design, fix this relationship. This idea imposes specific demands on chair design: the angle between the seat and the back should not be oblique. A chair that is angled more than 95 degrees (stated another way, the back is more than 5 degrees off vertical), sends the entire spine in a backward trajectory. No one can hold their head far back in space unsupported for long, so people bring their heads forward. With the spine going backward and the head going forward, the neck is forced into a swan-like configuration. This stresses the neck in a variety of different ways and contributes to the myriad problems imposed by bad use generally. (Note that if the angle between seat and back is great enough and the back fully extended to support the head, the chair technically speaking becomes a lounge, no longer a chair. Lounges have their own problems, especially if contoured, but usually provide more support and impose less distortion than classical right angle chairs.)

A second principle of the Alexander Technique is that the spine itself should not be deformed, which means that the two forward curves at the neck and lumbar should both be maintained, as should the two convex curves of the thoracic and sacral regions. This means that there should be a space hollowed out at the bottom of the chair back for the sacral region including the gluteus maximus. Without such "butt space" the pelvis is pushed forward and the lumbar curve flattens which tends to create a "C" shape slump for the spine as a whole rather than maintaining its elongated "S" shape. These distortions stress musculature, internal organs and spinal discs. On the whole, lumbar support contradicts the logic of the Alexander Technique. Lumbar support is used by ergonomic theorists in order to keep people's lower backs from rounding. For those with swayback or lordosis, of course, lumbar support is an obvious disservice, but even for others it reduces the overall tonus of the spine and spinal muscles and interferes with the balance between the two sets of curves.

The right angle seated posture is intrinsically stressful to the spine because thigh muscles affect the lumbar portion of the spine, pulling it backwards and sending it in the direction of a "C" shape slump. The only biomedical solution is not a better design of the components of the chair but rather reconfiguration of the chair itself to allow a fundamental change in posture. When the legs drop to a 135 degree angle below the spine rather than 90 degrees (in other words, when the upper leg is sloping down towards the floor), the work of sitting upright is distributed most evenly along the spine front to back and top to bottom. To take advantage of this physiological observation, the Norwegians invented the balance chair, also known as the posture chair or the kneeling chair and, more recently, as the computer chair. It is probably the most significant chair design of the 20th century because it is the first one to reconfigure fundamentally the basic elements of the chair, eliminating the back altogether, tilting the seat so radically that a knee rest is necessary to support the sitter. Lounge chairs also offer a 135 degree relationship between back and thigh, but the sitter's whole body is rotated differently in space.

An Alexander perspective leads us to be sympathetic to this idea that classical right-angle chair sitting is so problematic as to make designing a perfect chair impossible. At the same time, our experience with coordinated movement gives us clear directions for improving chairs. Although none is perfect, some chairs *are* better than others.

Alexander principles can direct the task of improving chair design. Planar as opposed to molded and shaped surfaces are such a contribution. Often designers contour chair seats to keep the pelvis from sliding forward, and they also contour the backs on the assumption that mimicking the shape of our rib cage is organic and therefore useful or comfortable. These ideas are mistaken. One of the insights from the rest position, which is such an integral component of the Alexander lesson and practice, is that lying on a firm surface gives the rib cage something to open out against and the spine something to lengthen along.

We always have to point out to our pupils that rest position cannot be accomplished satisfactorily in bed because mattresses are too soft, the body sinks in, the upholstery wraps around and we don't get the kind of opposition necessary for bones to open and separate; that is, we don't get the opposition necessary to create internal volume. This same sensory insight applies directly to seat design. The pelvic bowl, like the rib cage, needs to open out against a firm surface. Cupped seats, or overly upholstered seats, allow the sit bones to sink and pelvic wings to turn in towards themselves. Therefore, flat, planar surfaces for both seat and back are preferable to so-called organic. The organic curved seat backs also are intended to create stability so that it's easier to sit up without having to use muscle power, whereas using muscles in an overall pattern of coordinated effort would actually be better than not using them at all. Or, in automobiles, the justification is to keep the torso from rolling as the driver speeds around turns. But very few of us are race drivers in our cars, let alone in front of our computer terminals or telephones. The allusion to race car driving is a fantasy.

Another Alexander principle is that sensing the sit bones and the transfer of weight down to them is important. This not only reinforces the idea that the seat should be planar, but also indicates that it should be only lightly padded. Deep padding transfers weight to the muscles which compress the veins.

Weight is meant to be transferred through the bones, so excessive padding is counter-productive. In my experience a quarter to a half-inch of extremely firm foam, wool, felt or some other renewable resource is adequate. In the 19th century a quarter inch of horse hair was common.

An additional implication of the Alexander Technique concerns the feet. While Alexander principles give primacy to the freedom between head and neck, we also emphasize the importance of our feet yielding to gravity (as we maintain the integration of the back). Whether sitting or standing we want our feet on the floor, and ergonomicists concur, reporting that while 60% of the weight of sitting is transferred to the sit bones, another 40% is properly transferred to the heels. When the feet dangle from a chair that is too high, flesh under the thighs is cut, which hurts, muscle is forced into load bearing, which reduces circulation, and we lose the capacity to balance weight between the heels and the sit bones, which diminishes the stability of our spines. Therefore, the standard 18" chair height is inappropriate for over half the population. It really only suits tall adult men and women. What should be done? On the one hand, this observation argues for a lower seat height for conventional right angle seating. On the other hand, if one walks the sit bones out to the very edge of the chair and perches on the edge, then the higher the better because the sitter approaches the half sitting/half standing 3/4 height, 135 degree position discussed above. No matter which line of reasoning one pursues, both indicate that for conventional seating where the whole thigh rests on the seat, much more attention should be given to height than is routine. We should consider having chairs come in multiple sizes—Mama, Papa and Baby Bear sizes—and we should consider reintroducing foot stools as a standard piece of equipment to help people make up the difference between the height of the chair and the length of their own shinbones.

The most important insight from the Alexander Technique is that human beings are designed for movement and that more important than any single given posture is the quality of our movement, our overall coordination. Thus, movement should be promoted by design. Perhaps the most obvious way to do so is through a piece of furniture that moves, notably the good old-fashioned rocker. Rocking moves the ankles, knees, and hip sockets in obvious ways, and the head/neck joint and the entire spine in only slightly subtler ways. A less obvious way to create movement is the flat, planar surface. Its purpose is to allow the rib cage or the pelvic bowl or the spine to move—that is, to open and lengthen, so while the furniture itself is static, it facilitates movement within the body. Another way to introduce movement is by setting up different furniture configurations and then designing and orchestrating a path through them so one moves from one relatively static pose to another and the entire process exercises different sets of muscles and fluids, stresses different bones, and exercises different internal organs and sheets of fascia. In offices, for example, we could apply the idea of the exercise stations that are integrated into campuses and some parks. The office "par" course would include different workstations for working in different postures: standing, perching, sitting without back support, conventional sitting with back support, lounging with full back and head support, and even lying down in the fully horizontal position.

Desirable as this might be physiologically, movement may be at odds with management needs for control. Employers are often anxious that they would not be able to maximize employee productivity if they were to allow this kind of movement, but research shows that learning is improved with physical activity. In the end, the question is who has authority and where does it lie. The Alexander perspective suggests that the ultimate authority should be the body rather than the hierarchical social system of which it is a part.

This review of chair design demonstrates how the Alexander Technique can inform design, especially at the scale of the near-environment, that part that we touch with our bodies. While designing a perfect chair is impossible, the inevitable compromises can be made less arbitrary. The scientific principles imbedded in the Alexander Technique address all the significant issues in chair design—seat height, shape of front rail, cant of the seat, angle of back to seat, contour and upholstery, lumbar support, and movement—and other design problems are similarly informed by an Alexander perspective.

So, what about my life as a professor? The Alexander Technique has transformed it in several gratifying ways. First, of course, is the graduate seminar "Designing for the Near-Environment" mentioned earlier. Theoretical readings from sociology, history and anthropology establish the cultural regulation of the human body; experiential exercises in class each week heighten students's sensory awareness; and three design problems allow students to apply the premises of the Technique to shoes, chairs, and room interiors. Because I have modified my own "premises" over the years, I bring students to my house on a field trip to see what a domestic environment can look like when "Alexanderized." Some graduate students have singled out this course as the high point of their 2-3 years at Berkeley.

This material is popular with undergraduates as well—in my large survey class they rank those lectures on the chair and body-conscious design as my best. The topic also captured the interest of a literary agent, culminating in a recent book contract with W. W. Norton for the forthcoming publication of *The Chair: Rethinking Culture, Body, and Design.* In summary, my life as a professor has grown in depth and breadth because of the Alexander Technique. Two separate, and seemingly distant, fields have come together not only in the design of chairs, but also in my ability to profess something of general significance about the way our bodies meet the world in which we move.

Parallel Lives

❧ by Edward Avak

*Chi Wen Tzu used to think thrice before acting. The Master hearing of it
said, Twice is quite enough.*—Confucius

Switzerland, 1921. A young man is walking through a
forest crossed with paths. He is carrying paper, pencil,
and a book. It is a cool foggy morning. It clears the
mind. He stops at a picnic table, looks into his book, scribbles a
few notes, and moves on. A quarter of a mile farther on he
encounters a young couple. He recognizes them: a student staying at the same hotel where he lodges, and the student's fiancé.
He greets them politely and walks on. The next morning he
happens to meet them again at another point in the forest.

During the next few weeks he meets them repeatedly. He feels embarrassed. He doesn't want the couple to think he might be snooping, which he certainly is not. He had met them by accident. But, then again, how likely was it that they had met by accident and not on purpose? The question interests him. He goes back to the hotel and considers a simplified model of the paths through the forest—a grid of squares like city blocks, in an infinitely large city. He considers two points moving randomly along the streets of this infinite city, one point representing himself, the other the young couple. Is it likely that the two points will meet, given enough time? The problem is a difficult one. After several days he finds that the answer to his question is yes. He asks himself the same question again, but this time about two points moving in space through a grid of cubes. He finds that in this three dimensional case the points do not tend to meet, even in as much time as one would want. They tend to wander farther apart. Now he poses the question in the most general form—for a grid in an infinite dimensional space. He evolves a general theory and calls it the theory of "random walk." He is a mathematician. He is George Polya (1887-1985).

Australia, 1887. A young man is standing on a stage in front of a back-drop depicting a forest. The young man begins to recite lines from Shakespeare. He looks tense, his gestures are jerky and his voice sounds hoarse. After twenty minutes it becomes difficult for the audience to hear his voice. Some wonder if the young man is ill. The next night the same thing happens with a different audience. And the next night after that. The young man has by this time consulted a doctor, but to no avail. After a particularly bad night he returns to his lodgings at a hotel and wonders why he has a voice problem only when he performs. He decides to investigate this question by observing himself in mirrors while he rehearses in his hotel room. Progress is slow, but encouraging.

After several months he understands how to avoid the tensions which are interfering with his voice. But he sees a more general pattern at work. His voice is connected to his breathing habits, which in turn are connected to his habits of movement, which in turn are connected to his attitudes, his desires to accomplish something, and his sensory acuity. He finds that he can choose, consciously, to maintain a better general pattern which integrates these factors. He learns an immense amount about himself: How unwanted tensions arise, how constant vigilance is needed to rid himself of these habits, how easy it is to fool oneself. He has made discoveries of general importance, relevant to everyone. He has stumbled upon some of the prime factors of human coordination and consciously directed behavior. He is an artist who becomes an educator. He is F.M. Alexander (1869-1955).

Polya began on the path of his life in Hungary; Alexander began on his in Tasmania. If life were as uncomplicated as a two dimensional pattern we might have predicted a meeting between them. In fact they never met. But if they had would they have understood one another? Were they engaged in similar tasks during their lives? Who were these two men?

Towards the end of his career Polya sometimes played a game when he met children in his neighborhood near Stanford University. He liked to look down at the little boy or girl with great curiosity and ask, "Who are you?" They would invariably answer with a name, at which he would say, "Oh yes, of course, but that's only a name. I mean, who are you?" I wonder if any of those diminutive interlocutors ever countered with the same question. After all, that question may be, of all questions, the one most difficult to answer.

In Polya's case I can at least say that he was recognized during his life as one of the giants of twentieth century mathematics. However it is not his great technical achievements as a mathematician which impel me to write about him, but rather his pioneering work in the field of heuristics, the theory and art of problem solving, in this instance applied primarily to mathematics. His most elementary book in this field, *How to Solve It*, (1945), has sold more than a million copies and has been translated into fifteen languages. These statistics might alert us to the fact that the author may have been up to something more ambitious than the compilation of a primer. Indeed the book is an attempt to introduce even the innumerate or arithmophobic reader to the delights of mathematical discovery.

It is one of four books and a handful of articles in which Polya elaborated a set of techniques which a person interested in solving problems can use to stimulate ideas, to see connections, to produce and verify guesses. For example, before we can solve a non-trivial problem, we must make it our own. We must really want to solve it ourselves. Lack of motivation eliminates most problem solvers in the first round. Sound familiar? Next we must understand the problem. An obvious step, but it is surprising how often it is skipped with the result that we find no solution or a solution to the wrong problem. Then we need to see a connection between the data we have at hand and the goal we wish to reach, the "unknown" as we used to call it in school. Eventually, perhaps by considering auxiliary problems, or solving a simpler problem of the same type, we may evolve a plan for moving from the data to the unknown. Then the plan is carried out and the results checked. Procedures like these are explained in great detail with many examples.

Casually throwing off pithy aphorisms as he proceeds, Polya leads the reader step by step into the surprising forest of mathematics. No need for a trail of bread crumbs here. Once in, we don't want to leave. Heuristics will appeal to those of us who are puzzled and dissatisfied with solutions to problems that seem to be "pulled out of a hat" by an author. When confronted with these answers which "come out of the blue," we are left wondering how in the world the writer could have hit upon such an ingenious or profound or unexpected conclusion. If, on the other hand, an author displays his line of thought and in addition the procedures used to discover that line of thought, we are pleased and prepared for future excursions.

Now it is well known that creative thinking relies on subconscious mechanisms. The process of saturating the conscious mind with a problem and then waiting for an answer to "come up" from the subconscious is well documented. Moreover many creative individuals feel that they can stimulate the subconscious to provide material in a variety of ways—ranging from superstitious activities like always using a favorite pen to rationally conceived procedures based on generalizations from vast quantities of experience. A fine sense of balance is needed to steer a judicious course between the unpredictable depths of the subconscious and the heights of conscious technique. Too much emphasis on our dependence on the subconscious leads to ritualistic behavior; too much emphasis on step by step procedures leads to overly confident rigidity. Polya threads the course with finesse. "Let Us Teach Guessing," the title of one of his articles, balances the idea of a guess, which comes from who knows what subconscious source, and the idea of teaching, which implies the conscious transmission of technique and knowledge.

Polya once said that he took up mathematics because he thought he was not good enough for physics and too good for philosophy; mathematics seemed to be in between. The reader might gather as much from Polya's style of writing. When he does descend to philosophy in pointing out useful connections between mathematical heuristics and the conduct of life, he writes with clarity and brevity; what else should we expect from a mathematician? Some readers may be put off by transparently simple statements about life, even when they are profound and true. But some truths are inherently anticlimactic—rather than being final revelations, they are guides to be consulted frequently and from the very beginning. He begins one of his books with the words, "Experience modifies human belief. We learn from experience or, rather, we ought to learn from experience." Polya is quite aware of the ingenuousness of this kind of style, sometimes making wry comments on it, as when he writes, "First, we should be ready to revise any one of our beliefs. Second, we should change a belief when there is a compelling reason to change it. Third, we should not change a belief wantonly, without some good reason. These points sound pretty trivial. Yet one needs rather unusual qualities to live up to them. "(*Mathematics and Plausible Reasoning,* vol.1, p.8).

For Polya problem solving is an integral part of intelligent behavior. "Solving a problem means finding a way out of a difficulty, a way around an obstacle, attaining an aim which was not immediately attainable. Solving problems is the specific achievement of intelligence, and intelligence is the specific gift of mankind: solving problems can be regarded as the most characteristically human activity." (*Mathematical Discovery*, vol. 1, p.v). Polya is not alone in believing this. We see behind him not only the legions who created science but also craftsmen, cooks, carpenters, potters, poets and that host of people who have refined their skills partly through their dedication to solving the various problems which arise in their special activities. Who knows but that we might not find ourselves included in that latter group of people.

Admittedly, in "everyday life" we are not usually called upon to solve mathematical problems. Most people have problems of a different sort, ones more akin to those which confronted the man in the dream at the beginning of the *Pilgrim's Progress*, a lonely figure with a burden on his back, a book in his hand, weeping and lamenting as he cries out, "What shall I do?" That question reminds us of a realm of human existence where every deed bears its own particular fruit, where what we do or refrain from doing here and now will have tremendous importance later and elsewhere. Life sets us problems which are solved by actions and inactions. When we find an answer to this kind of problem, biologists say that we are displaying "intelligent behavior." They go on to say that this kind of behavior depends upon an array of keenly developed senses to provide us with what we need to know, i.e., the obstacles or general conditions under which we must solve the problem, and that it also depends on our ability to inhibit our immediate response long enough to decide upon a rational course of action. We seem, amazingly, to have the ability to make conscious choices, and this uncanny skill is part of what makes us human.

But Bunyan's conception of the human condition, a somber and moving one, in which the soul, weighed down by sin, seeks salvation, narrows our view. Problems are not always a burden. Sometimes we seek problems, and in solving the problems we have found or even created, we gain a deeper understanding of our world. As C. Judson Herrick has written, "The most significant characteristic of intelligence is the ability to invent problems." (*The Evolution of Human Nature*, 1956, p. 359). I once asked a mathematician who shared my enthusiasm for Polya whether he actually made use of Polya's methods when he was solving problems. Alas, he said that in fact he didn't, because he found solving problems relatively easy. What he found difficult was finding important problems to solve. The theory of problem solving is as old as Euclid. Polya holds his place in a long line of eminent explorers in this field—Descartes, Leibniz, Euler and Bolzano. We have yet to see the birth of a theory of problem inventing.

Some people are lucky enough to have a problem thrust

upon them whose solution bears on a wide area of human experience. A man in Australia has a sore throat and gets over it; end
of story. However, by the time F.M. Alexander had gotten over
his sore throat he had solved one of the greatest and most general of problems in human experience, one which had gone
unnoticed because it is the very medium in which we move—
everyday activity. I can imagine the looks of surprise, if not
consternation, with which a reader unacquainted with
Alexander's work might greet the idea that everyday activity
constitutes a problem. Perhaps those whose lives are spent in
back-breaking servitude, or pain, or illness, would find such an
idea plausible. Getting through the day is indeed a problem for
many such people. But we tend to consider these cases as special. Normally everyday activity doesn't deserve much thought,
we believe, even though the bald expression of that opinion
comes embarrassingly close to the notion that how we live our
lives doesn't deserve investigation. In any case, it would seem to
be an abuse of language to call everyday activity, la vie quotidienne,
a problem, or a difficulty, or an obstacle blocking the achievement of our aims. Alexander found otherwise. He discovered
that the manner in which he spoke in ordinary circumstances
and the similarly strained way in which he performed his
activities constituted the primary source of his voice problem.
This was a major discovery.

The golfer misses his shot if he takes his eyes off the ball.

Obviously he needs to work on his form. It is less obvious that form plays an equally important role in the ordinary activities of life. Like many great discoveries, Alexander's was a discovery of the obvious. We know we function better when we take our time. Eating too quickly, driving too fast, rushing through a carpentry project, we can usually predict the result; but we never stop to consider the implications of these common experiences. F.M. Alexander noticed something that no one had noticed before, the connection between what he came to call "the use of the self" and the standard of our functioning. Flesh is heir to some ills, but not all; some seem to be earned, and earned by diligent practice. Whether we recognize it or not, that practice is unceasing and is the basis of habits, both good and bad. Decades before the term became fashionable, Alexander had discovered the basis of human stress.

Alexander found a solution to that problem. It lay in the exercise of the human ability to inhibit one's immediate impulse to get something done in the habitual way long enough to decide what ought to be done and how to do it with minimal effort and maximal flexibility and control. The reader will notice the similarity between this procedure and the biologist's definition of intelligent behavior alluded to earlier. Alexander called this process "constructive conscious control." Indeed much of what Alexander spent his life teaching was simply consciously guided intelligent behavior. Going even further than those who see conscious life as a small patch on a vast canvas of subconscious activity, Alexander conflated the subconscious and the habitual, thus rendering that patch even smaller. If we are not fully conscious when we act habitually, then we are hardly ever fully conscious at all. A philosopher once told me that he felt lucky if he was able to think in a non-habitual way for about one minute per day. He would have understood Alexander's rigorous standards for consciousness.

It is this uncompromising view of conscious life that makes Alexander's idea at once revolutionary and unappealing to most people. It is revolutionary because it challenges the old model of human beings as conscious, rational creatures who need once in a while to resort, through various techniques or rituals, to the sub/superconscious. On the contrary, Alexander considered the human species to be at a turning point which demanded the cultivation of a type of conscious behavior rarely seen thus far and very likely to be lost through disuse in the future. His views are also unappealing because few people enjoy having their collusion in their own undoing pointed out. Here is a man who invites us simply to consider what we can refrain from doing as a basis for solving our problems. This is an exercise in sobriety which has limited allure. We would rather continue on a wrong course of action and then make appeals to external powers to save us, an age-old strategy which has made use of everything from prayer, trance, dreaming, ritual and magic to hypnotism, autosuggestion, biofeedback, brainwashing and drugs. All these invocations of "greater powers" would have called to Alexander's mind the retort of Hotspur to Glendower's boast that he could call spirits from the vasty deep: "Why, so can I, or so can any man; But will they come when you do call for them?" *(Henry IV,* pt.i, ii.iv). And if they do come, do they come as angels, devils or ignes fatui? Or, perhaps more ominously, as distractions.

The alternative of conscious living lies along another path, which, although it leads towards a richer array of choices, passes through and depends upon the vast unconscious metabolic world which supports our very lives and all our abilities. While recognizing our capacity to move along that path as itself one of the supernal gifts of nature, it is a gift that demands to be perfected.

The fruits of consciously directed living are sometimes surprising. For example, elegance and spontaneity are usually contrasted with conscious choice, yet the royal road to elegance and spontaneity for humans is prolonged conscious deliberation. I use the word "deliberation" advisedly. The root meaning of the word is to ponder, to consider alternatives, or, as I would like to put it, to use the imagination in combinatorial play as an aid to choosing the best form of behavior. Deliberation leads naturally to liberation from the stereotypical. After a lifetime spent observing animal behavior, the ethologist Konrad Lorenz suspected that many animals have a drive to perfect the elegance and efficiency of their behavior patterns, a drive towards grace, or, as Alexander called it, "good use." Animal play may be more than token aggression or defense; it may be a kind of behavioral solfège, a primitive artistic practice directed toward the achievement of some dimly descried perfection of form and balance. In humans this play can take place mentally, as prelude to action. Perhaps it is not a coincidence that it took an actor like Alexander, a player of roles, to make the discoveries he did.

What may come as a surprise is that Alexander's "constructive conscious control" depends upon a subtle mastery of certain muscular patterns that modulate our relationships to the external world and to gravity. Physiologists call these patterns "postural and orienting reflexes," and some see in them the germ of all intelligent behavior.

From muscular reflex to conscious intelligence may seem like quite a leap. But consider the opinions of a few eminent scientists. For example, Dr. Arnold Gesell writes, "Thought processes depend upon antecedent postural responses and are indeed rarefied revivals of these responses." *(Embryology of Behavior,* 1945, p.46). More specifically, Lorenz writes, "The movement which orients the animal in space can never be an innate instinctive pattern, since the necessary coordination can of course not be determined in the special form required for any individual situation. The orienting movement is the most primitive and most penetrating form of non-instinctive behavior in the behavioral system...This behavior cannot be distinguished from behavior controlled by the simplest form of insight." ("The Establishment of the Instinct Concept," 1937, in *Studies in Animal and Human Behavior*, 1970, vol.1, p. 273). In other words, we cannot act intelligently, insightfully, in a situation, until we have taken in that situation and our relationship to it. We take in a situation by physically turning our heads and looking at it, by orienting ourselves in relation to it, by considering the uniqueness of our plight. Only by stopping and taking the time to exercise such unruffled circumspection can we cultivate the ability to respond in a more intelligent fashion to the world around us. Significantly, the world in-forms us; it does not simply trigger an innate instinctive pattern. The world contributes to the nature of the patterns which are in the process of being established in us, and our intelligent responses to the world partly determine the stimuli to which we are going to respond. Orientation is not a blind reaction. It is a circuit which allows the flow of information and activity in both directions between the individual and the world. If the orienting functions suffer damage or interference, then so does our standard of intelligent behavior. Conversely, if our conscious awareness of the environment flags, the orienting mechanism weakens.

Although I have referred to a physician who vaguely suggests that thinking is a ghostly acting, and to an ethologist who believes that the particular kind of thinking we associate with intelligence and insight is an outgrowth of a particular kind of muscular action, the orienting response, their comments lack the cogency which a detailed description of the linkage between intelligent behavior and the muscular system would provide. However, a couple of specific examples might be more illuminating than a treatise on the neurophysiology of intelligence.

Alexander once said that the most difficult principle of his work to understand was that change, psychophysical change, was to be brought about by "thought alone." This idea, which might be mistaken as an endorsement of mind-body dualism, was uttered on the contrary in full confidence that not only were thought and body inextricably intertwined but that pure thought was our surest means for establishing the possibility of non-habitual behavior. Alexander's voice problem seemed on the surface to be a muscular problem. Deeper analysis showed it to be a primarily mental problem, encompassing such issues as ends and means, causality, the timing and coordination of activity, the need for skepticism with regard to sense impressions, the inhibition of habitual behavior patterns, and finally the proper role of conscious control in human behavior, a role, by the way, that must be played with tact, without overbearing meddling in the details of activity and yet bravely enough to dominate either impulsiveness or directionless drift. It was by thinking these issues through that the recovery of his voice was finally brought about.

A second example is provided by none other than Albert Einstein. In 1945 the mathematician Jacques Hadamard wrote a classic study called *The Psychology of Invention in the Mathematical Field*, which summarized the results of a survey he conducted among the leading mathematicians of his day to find out how they obtained their ideas and solved their scientific problems. With one notable exception, he found that mathematicians thought of their problems either visually, with the aid of imaginary spatial and geometric patterns, or, on the other hand, algebraically, with the aid of imagined algebraic symbolism and logical relations of implication. They either "saw" the problem, or they "calculated" the problem symbolically.

The one notable exception who did not fit neatly into Hadamard's two part classification was Einstein. He wrote to Hadamard, "Words or language, as they are written or spoken, do not seem to play any role in my mechanism of thought. The psychical entities which seem to serve as elements in thought are certain signs and more or less clear images which can be "voluntarily" reproduced and combined....The above mentioned elements are, in my case, of visual and some of *muscular type.*"

Here we have a third category and a salient example of thinking with one's muscles. There are several popular accounts of Einstein's theories which describe him as a youth wondering what it would be like to ride a light beam. The fruit of these youthful meditations was the Special Theory of Relativity. Certainly that ride would have been both a visual and a muscular thrill. This anecdote derives from an autobiographical note he wrote in 1956: "If one runs after a light wave with [a velocity equal to the] light velocity, then one would encounter a time-independent wavefield. However, something like that does not seem to exist." I am told that we non-physicists can take that to mean that if one followed a light particle at its own speed, we should expect it to appear to stand still; yet there is no experimental evidence of a light particle at rest. No matter how fast we run and in whatever direction, those little glimmers are moving at a disorienting speed of 186,000 miles per second! But by redefining length and time, by recalibrating the tools with which one measures speeds (shades of the muscle spindles?), he was able to develop a theory which accounted for the experimental evidence. He brought his muscular intuitions in line with the facts of the situation. And those intuitions and the changes in the laws of physics entailed by them proved to be surprisingly different from what we feel they should be.

Einstein's brief statements about his creative processes tantalize us. We would like to know more about them, but their sources are hidden. There is a well-known picture of the participants in the 1927 Solvay Conference of physicists. Einstein sits in the middle of the front row, around him sit and stand many of the leading physicists in the world at that time. One of his hands rests on his leg, palm up, the other hangs relaxed at his side. He is the only one who looks truly calm, and in that state of balance which Alexander called "going up"—poised mentally and physically in the gravitational field that he studied for much of his life. I like to think that Alexander was a co-worker in the same study, but with a different orientation—Einstein working on the mathematical description of gravity, Alexander on the consequences of living in a world where every decision is potentially weighty.

Even though the link between Alexander and Einstein may seem a tenuous one, at least it is a muscular one. When we come to consider Alexander and Polya, the relations between them are more abstract but clearer. Alexander and Polya were both masters of the art of self-reflection, of the art of being able to engage in some skillful activity and at the same time to watch oneself and come to an understanding of how that activity was brought about. Rather than simply becoming a good actor in the one case or a good mathematician in the other, they were interested in the means whereby they accomplished what they did. Their focus on *how* they functioned is characteristic of the post-Galilean movement in science. Whether this recent trend in science is better than the older tradition of posing ontological questions to nature is moot. What is clear is that some people simply find more satisfaction in knowing what things are, while others are drawn towards a knowledge of how things behave. Polya and Alexander wanted to know how! Furthermore, when they found out, they invited others to share in their knowledge. They invited others into their workshops, messy as they might be, to see how it was done. For both of them the esoteric was execrable. They displayed their mistakes, their fruitless wanderings as well as the meandering evolution which finally led to successful results.

Most mathematicians, poets, philosophers, or performing artists prefer to present their final works to the public without the least trace of the workshop clinging to them, usually with good reason. In this way they astound, but they also discourage. How in the world could I ever think of such a theorem or poem, develop such unexpected philosophical arguments or play the piano with such consummate skill? But Alexander invites us into one of the most profound personal histories ever written, revealing all the steps and missteps, every conjecture and every experiment he performed until he finally made the discoveries he did. The result is a theory and a practice which stand on their own legs, legs like our own, instead of floating four feet above our heads. Similarly Polya allows us to see how curiosity about some question can lead to experimenting with numbers, looking for patterns, making conjectures, correct ones and incorrect ones, searching, testing, and generalizing until one discovers a truth. What they did, they did by exercising honesty, self-criticism, and experimentation. What they did can be repeated by others. Is that a definition of science?

Curiously, both men disdained inspiration as a basis for sound teaching. Alexander distrusted a dependence on inspiration in teaching because he viewed it as undependable, a temporary enthusiasm in the learner easily displaced by the next emotional gust and possibly dangerous to an unstable mind. Polya ignored the role of inspiration because he wanted his methods to be teachable, and inspiration cannot be taught.

Finally their achievements depended on their great technical skills—Polya's virtuosity as a master mathematician, Alexander's fabulous skill in conveying with his hands a poise and freedom virtually unattainable through an individual's solitary efforts. Although such a level of skill is a necessary condition for being a great teacher, it is not sufficient. They had more. In Alexander's case, people remember his poise, his clearsightedness and his ability to convey to his students a sense of ever expanding possibilities. Polya, in his turn, was able to develop in the student powers of insight he or she did not know were there. And they both welcomed company on their walks, walks which were always adventures of discovery.

A Two Wheel Essay

❧ *by Barry Collins*

Cycling predates the Alexander Technique in my life by many years. Although my older brother was a keen cyclist, I didn't have much more than a passing interest as a youngster. It was only when my wife and I were driving back from Greece one year that we were drawn to the display window of a big German department store: small wheeled folding bikes were on sale for the U.K. equivalent of £5. For that price we couldn't resist. So we bought two, and put them in the car. That was the thin end of the wedge.

From there we went to off-the-peg "proper" bikes, and then on to custom made frames, adorned with the best bits of kit from France, Japan and Italy. For us (and I include my wife here), it was bikes and travelling, not mortgages and children, that were our personal paths of growth and development. But despite the many aches and pains that can come from cycling, it was the pressures and strains of being a practicing dentist that first drew me to the Alexander Technique.

I survived the first ten years of General Practice dentistry modestly well, but then, quite suddenly, a chasm of nervous tension opened up. The inherited nervous disposition from my dear mother, plus the effects of doing close and detailed work on patients, nearly all of whom were in various states of fear and tension, were having a devastating impact. No patient enjoys a visit to the dentist; there is that sense of free floating anxiety that goes with the first smell of a dental surgery. Well, my job as a practitioner (although this was never spelled out at dental school) is to "stay back" from this air of anxiety. I am supposed to be caring and supportive, but not to get emotionally involved. In hindsight I could "do" all of the rest, but I could not maintain that healthy distance. If you are not capable of doing this, you just get sucked into the almost palpable morass of anxiety and tension, that is there from the beginning to the end of a working day.

Seemingly, the patient's response became my response. As a result, the jointed surfaces of my right arm became virtually welded together with tension. I became so fearful of causing pain or discomfort that on occasion I could do almost nothing at all. Working a full day became a nightmare. My heart rate would go through the roof, and I would sweat and tremble. Nowadays these symptoms are recognized as a panic attack. I would even hang by my fingertips from the door frame, in an attempt to bring some relief from the locked up arm joints. All I did was make my muscles even tighter.

My doctor had nothing to offer me, except an operation on my elbow, and/or a course of Valium. Unlike F.M. Alexander's realization that the problems plaguing him were of his own making, I didn't say, "What is it that I am doing to myself to create this problem?" I just sensibly said good-bye to my doctor. And then, by chance, I stumbled on Dr. Wilfred Barlow's paperback on the Alexander Technique, read it greedily, and found an Alexander teacher.

Taking lessons at this stage brought me no wondrous insights or miraculous changes. They were really no more than a safety valve to keep me from being swallowed up by this giant black hole of tension. I had no body understanding of this thing my teacher called direction; it was all I could do to grip wildly at not tightening—if this is not too paradoxical a concept. My teacher must have despaired but never showed it. He was always very supportive (and this attitude is something that has helped me greatly in my own teaching). Even now I read with awe descriptions by those fortunate folk who have had transcendent experiences after one or two lessons. What was it these people "had" that I didn't, except my tension perhaps?

It was only a considerable time into my Alexander reeducation that I began applying the Technique to cycling. Especially so, during the daily ride from home to Alexander training school, to dental practice and back to home. Three years of cycling 20 miles a day gave me plenty of thinking time—thinking time not only for my manner of cycling, but also for all of the discoveries being made at my Alexander school. In hindsight, those three 40 minute rides each day gave me the space and time to make those connections to my own life that for a long time were just printed words in Alexander's books.

Even so, the wider implications of the Technique have taken time in developing for me. When I read Anatomist Raymond Dart's paper on the "Significance of Skill," I saw cycling in a different light. Perhaps because I have been a cyclist for many years, I never considered it a skill. But as Dart says, "All muscular and mental collaboration entails the exercise of skill...skilled movement connotes skilled living; i.e. art!" Some people might not be too happy with this definition of art, but I do know that for myself watching any activity that is carried out in an easy and fluid way is very pleasing to the eye—and ease and fluidity do depend upon muscular and mental coordination. This pattern of coordination is the same thing that had gone haywire in my early dentistry. The easy coordination of my youth seemingly evaporated under the strains of my work. The last 20 years have been spent recapturing it, or at least slowly learning the process by which this coordination is made possible.

Recently, I read a letter to the editor of a cycling magazine, regarding the source of our ability actually to stay upright on a bike. The answers were all distinctly unsatisfactory, and had me puzzled. Thinking this through, I came to the conclusion that balancing on a bike is an extension of learning to be in balance while in standing, with a few extra joints involved, plus movement possibilities added on below the sitting bones and the feet. A better question in retrospect would have been, "Why *can't* some people balance on two wheels?" Without doubt, the momentum of the bike does mask interfering muscle tension patterns, but riding very slowly or even staying upright while stationary is possible. Balance demands freely movable body joints, which are dependent upon correct muscle tone. If you observe a cyclist closely, you can see how their particular tension patterns are affecting their riding.

In fact, these tension patterns can be seen at even the highest levels of cycling. For me, watching the Tour de France on television each July is both educational and compulsive. Here is skill and elite fitness in peak form. If the rider is going well, the upper part of the body is relatively still in the saddle; the torso is usually stretched out beyond the front of the handle bars, using extension pieces known as triathlon bars (innovated by the American Greg LeMond). The rider's legs (if viewed in slow motion via the wonders of modern video), can be seen to be led by the heels. Watching this action on the screen gives me a sense of the leg opening out, rather than simply pushing—the leg "simply pushing" being a rather frantic overuse of muscle power, driving the rider up out of his saddle, rather than the bike forward; while the leg "opening out" implies a sophisticated delivery of power, in tune with bike speed, road demands, and race tactics. Anatomically, I think of it as a full extension of the front of the hip joint, and the back of the knee joint, but with a relative resilience to the front of the ankle joint; all this is going on at the same time that the torso is releasing up and away from the contact with the saddle. So it is not just the leg, but the whole body "opening out," each part relative to the other.

Of all of the leg joints, the ankle is probably the most significant. The freer the ankle, the more the rider stays in the saddle, whereas the progressively less resilient the ankle becomes, the more the rider rises out of the saddle, finally coming right up over the front wheel for power sprinting and hill climbing. The French, in their inimitable way, call this position "en danceurs." As the pedals are integrally joined to the shoes these days, the sensation of leaning out over the front wheel is like running into the wind with a bicycle strapped to your feet. This progressive ankle "stiffening" is a marker for all of the body joints; they all will respond similarly to create a "solid" but still moveable structure for pure power delivery.

So the top bike riders have developed qualities of poise and balance and freedom that would be instantly recognized and appreciated by an Alexander teacher. But as easy also to recognize is when things start to go wrong. With loss of rhythm, the rider's body starts to sway from side to side. The back is no longer solidly supported on the saddle, but is being "pulled down" on each up stroke of the leg. The back begins to look a bit like a sagging table. This pulling down is a contraction down the whole front of the body, the rider using these muscles as a poor substitute for legs that are probably incredibly tired. The irony is that with the loss of the back for support, the legs will have that much less power—power transmission is dependent upon a relatively rigid structure, otherwise the power is dissipated into twisting the back, and not turning the pedals. Maybe the reason for the loss of coordination is a simple loss of concentration, with thoughts of the winner's rostrum causing the rider to forget the best means towards this desired end. Or maybe the culprit is a more fundamental lack of ability to control the pace. Again as Dart says, "Perfect relaxation of unwanted muscles is the key to skilled performance."

A skilled performance on a downhill run can be equally staggering to watch. The cyclist can reach speeds of 70mph. During these moments the bike and rider seem to merge together as one. At those speeds the finger width tires occasionally hit unexpected gravel, and the rider can go down in the blink of an eyelid. But occasionally the rider responds even quicker than the eyelid, and if the video is watching at that moment, then the response almost seems to merge with the stimulus. This is quite magical. The time scale indicates that only a thought on the part of the rider keeps him in balance, particularly at these high speeds. This could perhaps be described as a whole-of-body-and-mind response, but of the smallest proportions. The rider will go down if the response is inappropriately too large or too small.

Now, I have never taught the Technique to a pro rider (although this would be a fascinating project), but I have spent many hours working on myself in the saddle. Like the professional rider, I too am looking for efficiency of movement, aiming to keep the volume of effort down but the momentum up. A way has got to be found of improving and strengthening muscular coordination, without losing flexibility. However, when I'm cycling and feeling tired, or perhaps conversely feeling strong and a bit competitive, I find that my coordination goes to pot; I notice that I am sliding forward in the saddle; that I am, in fact, pulling myself towards the handlebars by over using my stomach and biceps muscles, and rounding my back in typical cyclist fashion. If I continue in this mode for very long I really can do myself an injury.

I remember, in particular, making one journey home from central London. I was just starting the one big hill climb of the ride when there was a tinkle of a polite bell, and an elderly gentleman (even in relation to me) sailed past on an ancient sit-up-and-beg bicycle. I felt that the gauntlet had been thrown down. Good use was chucked aside; egos had locked horns because I was riding the latest bit of kit here; state of the art clad in lycra, versus Edwardian gentility. At the top of the hill it was neck and neck, but the old guy didn't give an inch...and we both suffered; he probably went to intensive care to have his first coronary, and I certainly to my friendly osteopath, to have my back reshaped.

What had happened? Looking back I realize that at that moment I had lost my ability to "prevent the wrong." Overexcitement of the race caused me to think only of winning and to forget my coordination.

The fizz of adrenaline has really got a lot to answer for. Only old familiar patterns of movement seemed relevant to this situation, because of a giant expansion of my ego, coupled with an instant shrinkage of my brain. I doubt whether I could have gone any faster by keeping my coordination, but I don't know; certainly I would have survived the encounter intact, which wasn't so that afternoon.

The dental equivalent of this story is that unless I keep my brain in gear, and my coordination somewhat organized during treatment sessions, I may still be "blown away" by events; extremely nervous patients cause alarm bells to ring, and red lights to flash in my head, warning me to take care, as there is danger ahead. I must still consciously keep space between me and them, and stay well coordinated, and then I am able to "be there" for them without hurting myself. My original problems of some 20 years ago are now nearly totally under control. With the benefit of hindsight, I must say that without the insight acquired with the Alexander Technique, I would never have regained the controls and centeredness that I can now organize for myself.

Unlike in dental surgery where the arm tension problem can still show itself if I'm not paying attention, loss of coordination on the bike always comes out as exquisite pain in the lower lumbar region, from which I usually take at least a week to recover. That gives me plenty of time to reflect....

One of the reasons my arm is not a problem on the bike is that I quite consciously do *not* grip the handlebars, only resting my hands and arms on the brake levers and allowing the weight of my upper body to be supported by the heels of my hands. When I need to rise up out of the saddle to climb a steep hill, it is a pleasant sensation not to grip the bars to "steady the bike," but to allow it to flick more freely left and right in response to each pedal stroke.

To have a sense of how much contact is actually needed between hands and handlebars, it is an interesting game to practice riding the bike "no hands." My advice is to find a quiet and gently sloping road, build up a little speed, and then try easing back and up off of the bars altogether. It doesn't take very much practice to find yourself sitting very upright on the saddle, steering the bike by weighting up either one sitting bone, or the other. Neither is it too difficult to peddle the bike while swinging your arms, as if in walking. The next stage is to pivot forward delicately from the hip joints, and to allow the hands to rest lightly back on the bars. The light and free support that the hands provide in this way encourages a better use of the legs and back.

One of the areas where I have been most able to explore the effects of good coordination and the ways in which we interfere with it, is in my stationary training bike sessions. It has shed light for me on one of the most common problems for cyclists—the tendency to pull downwards and forwards while riding.

Using the stationary bike, it is not too difficult to sense that the powerful supporting muscles of the back are being interfered with by the stomach and biceps getting overactive, pulling me down towards the handlebars, rather than allowing the legs to release away towards the pedals. In this pulling down mode, the ball of the foot plays its part as well. It is virtually impossible to stay supported by the saddle when the front of the foot is pushing away, because for the ball of the foot to push, the ankle has to stiffen, and when the ankle stiffens the whole body is pushed up and out of the saddle, the hands grab the handlebars and the front of the torso is pulled down. Now when the heel leads the movement, the ankle stays soft and released, and the torso can stay supported. The intention is to avoid bracing specific "bits" of oneself, and to spread the load among the pedals, bars, and saddle. If one starts bracing at low speed, there is no chance of easing off at higher speeds.

Slow speed cycling on my stationary bike has confirmed to me the value of the outside edge of the heel as the best focal point of leg extension. This mental direction keeps the knees from being drawn inwards towards each other, and again allows the sitting bones to be supported by the saddle. Interestingly, even when I am paying as much attention as I can to these coordination patterns, my saddle still gets twisted to the right of center after a long ride—empirical proof that some asymmetric twists are going on, causing me to overuse one side of my body. All of this seems to me to be very much an unflattering working example of Raymond Dart's observation of the way that muscles spiral around the body. A close observation on my part has shown me that I still pull my left knee inwards on the down stroke, pulling the left sitting bone forward and so twisting the saddle to the right.

Of course it won't come as any surprise to people initiated into the Alexander Technique to read that it is the whole body that is involved in these compressive pulling down patterns; but it does come as a big insight when one can analyze these patterns for oneself. Especially so when one is involved in activities of increasing muscular effort. Without doubt, the greater the physical demand being made, the louder the internal volume of internal direction that is needed, because it is just so easy to pull down and into yourself to get that little bit extra. But what you get is not always what you want. The end result of "trying too hard" is not always increased speed and power.

On a fairly recent ride, this understanding was brought home to me quite energetically. My wife and I were out in the country just north of London, and towards the end of the ride I was unfortunate enough to have my gear cable shear off, leaving me only with top gear, the least suitable for short and steep hills. The pedals became very hard to push and I lost my cool. I was "pushing" the pedals thoughtlessly, (e.g. tightening my ankles, and using the balls of my feet, and my toes), and was generally thinking nasty thoughts of cycles and cycling. The more tired I became, however, the more I managed to calm down and get my brain back into gear. With this change in attitude came an immediate improvement. The sensible way to deal with this problem was to spread intentionally the load as evenly as possible throughout the body, keeping all of my joints as resilient and as unclenched as possible, commensurate with using just enough overall effort to keep the bike upright and moving. Again, in the conventional wisdom, I was spreading the load evenly between pedals, bars and saddle. It all turned into a very pleasant experience.

Alexander work is often mistakenly considered to be only possible when one is upright, and as effortlessly free as possible. But there are occasions, like the above incident, where one has to put in vast amounts of effort. This effort has to be directed, with intention, to keep the tightness patterns to a minimum. Nurturing this internal direction is not too difficult to maintain when conditions are not too stressful, but becomes increasingly more difficult as the level of demand increases.

Keeping the whole of the body even modestly well organized while cycling takes a lot of thinking and a lot of strong intention. The hands, for example, should be used for just quietly supporting the upper body, for operating the brake levers, and for avoiding London's pot-holes. But this, unfortunately, is not so for most recreational cyclists, who, instead, use the hands to grip, and to pull downward and forwards. This bad use is compounded by a sense of a mythical joint at the level of the seventh cervical vertebra, from which the head is in turn pulled downward and backwards.

Ultimately, the real endeavor is to allow the legs to move, without having to tighten unnecessarily through the ribs, abdomen, shoulders, neck or anywhere else. Paradoxically, working this way shifts the emphasis away from overusing a particular part of the body to a better use of the whole body during any activity.

Cycling, by its very nature, is a sport based upon efficiency. Anybody who has spent some time servicing their own bike is familiar with that silky fluid feeling that the bike then gives; it has less gritty interferences, more freshly lubed bearing surfaces...it feels rattle free, more connected and more of a piece.

A well tuned bike and a "well tuned" rider combine to produce a very pleasing example of efficiency in motion.

I remember well one glorious ride, in the company of my dear wife, along the banks of the Loire river in France. It was a golden spring afternoon, and we had about 10 miles to go after a longish ride; we were tired but somehow we both found this magical steady rhythm, a sort of cycling version of lengthening and widening. There was a sense of energy being created rather than energy consumed, and the net effect was exhilaration rather than weariness.

For me, this was the very embodiment of the Alexander Technique.

Floating Thoughts

✑ *by Deborah Caplan*

I am sure my mind is much like other people's: full of floating thoughts. In my professional life I have two main sets
of floating thoughts—those arising from my experience
with the Alexander Technique, and those originating from my
work as a physical therapist. I cherish both these areas of
knowledge, and am continually enchanted by how well they
intertwine and compliment one another.

When I am giving an Alexander lesson, "Alexander"
thoughts are in the foreground. This means that I have an
awareness of my own use, as well as that of my student, in

terms of breathing, head-neck-torso integration, ease of movement and directed energy. However, I may also have "physical therapy" thoughts, such as ideas for specific strengthening or stretching exercises, rising to the surface during the same lesson. These thoughts will be more focused on a particular area of the body my student is having problems with, such as an injured knee, or a spinal curvature, or a disc problem in the neck or low back. But these two conceptual approaches are not in conflict, for even though I may give my student specific exercises, I will also explain that improving the use of the whole self is the best way of achieving healing in any one specific area. I will often refer to Alexander's own experience of needing to improve the use of his whole self in order to solve his voice problem.

My first exposure to Alexander's work was when I was ten years old. At that time my mother became a certified teacher of the Alexander Technique, and I had my first lessons with F.M. Alexander. These lessons took place in a small school Mr. Alexander started in Stowe, Massachusetts. It was quite strange having a mother who taught the Technique in the 1940's. Neither the general public nor the medical profession were knowledgeable about mind-body disciplines at that time. So, deep down in my thoughts, I regarded my mother's work as strange and secretly wished she were more like other mothers.

That attitude started to change because of dance—my great love when I was young. I first studied classical ballet, taking classes daily. Many of the classes were "on point," an aesthetic requirement most ruinous to the feet and all other body parts. My mother allowed me to pursue this passion provided I took Alexander lessons at the same time. I soon found that the principles of the Alexander Technique were helping me tremendously in dance class. I achieved excellent balance on point and great jumping power.

From classical ballet I went on to modern dance. Through both high school and college I performed and taught modern dance. My early lessons with F.M. Alexander and then with Lulie Westfeldt helped keep me leaping high and injury free during this period of intensive dancing.

While I was going to college, my mother trained me to become a teacher of the Alexander Technique. For three years she worked with me and supervised my working with her students. I have no memory of a discussion with her in which I was given a choice to say "yea" or "nay" to this training. It just sort of happened. Strange as it may seem, I took to the training with ease and no feeling of rebellion (the rebellion was to come later). When my mother died in 1953 her students kept coming to me for lessons. So there I was, a teacher of the Alexander Technique.

When I think back to that period in my life I realize that my mother, the Alexander Technique, and I were all somehow entwined. The entwining was comfortable for me and I certainly enjoyed the teaching, but my sense of having my own identity had been compromised.

During my last year of college, one of my classmates was in a serious car accident. While visiting her in the hospital I learned for the first time about the profession of physical therapy. I fell passionately in love with this profession and decided that this was to be my chosen life's work. My passion came from two sources: my need to rebel against my mother and her work, and my desire, since childhood, for knowledge about how the body is made and functions: What are we like inside and how do we work?

I did not see physical therapy as connected in any way to the Alexander Technique. Different profession. Different approaches. Different thoughts. I would go back to school and take classes in anatomy, physiology and the nervous system. I would learn how to teach exercises, and use equipment that electrically stimulated muscles or gave heat to injured parts of the body. I would teach people to walk with braces and crutches and artificial limbs. This was completely different from my training and activities as a teacher of the Alexander Technique. Indeed, it involved a very different thinking process and way of looking at the body. But most important, I had discovered physical therapy, and developed a passion for it, on my own.

I continued teaching the Alexander Technique while I fulfilled the academic requirements for my new profession. However, once I began working full time in a hospital as a physical therapist, I completely stopped my Alexander teaching. I also stopped referring to myself as a teacher of the Technique. My desire to be a physical therapist was so strong that I did not want to be identified with any other profession. I wanted to enter the world of physical therapy with a fresh, open self, to better explore the wonders of this new world.

But I cheated! I was not teaching Alexander's work to others, but every moment of every day that I was in that hospital working with patients, I applied the Alexander principles to myself (I was thinking those floating thoughts of Alexander). As with my dancing, I know my knowledge of the Alexander Technique helped me avoid injury. Physical therapy is a very physically demanding and strenuous profession. Most physical therapists eventually reach the point of having neck, shoulder and back pain themselves because of the nature of the work they do. The thought processes and the procedures involved in physical therapy, valuable as they are for the patient, do not protect the physical therapist.

But eventually, the inevitable happened: After several years of hospital work in which I personally derived benefit from my knowledge of the Alexander Technique, but did not pass these benefits on to others, I began to see how the Alexander

Technique could be of tremendous therapeutic value to some of the patients I was treating. I guess my need to rebel against my mother had been satisfied. I could once again include the work she had done as part of my professional self. I therefore made the decision to leave the hospital and return to giving lessons in the Alexander Technique.

When I was practicing physical therapy in a hospital, many of my patients had back problems. Now, as a teacher of the Alexander Technique, I have chosen to work with people with similar problems. I mainly give lessons to those who have a significant medical history of musculoskeletal distress. This allows me to realize my first passion, which is to teach Alexander, and use my second passion, physical therapy, as a valuable source of additional healing information.

As I look back on the many lessons I have given to people in pain, I think of myself as the bearer of good news. Inherent in Alexander's teachings is information concerning the body that dispels a lot of negative thinking about the human condition. Many new students come for lessons already programmed by their physicians and by society to think a whole basket of negative thoughts about themselves: "I am degenerating! My doctor tells me I have degenerative disc disease." "My back will always hurt because I walk upright on two feet." "There is no way I can win against the downward force of gravity." Such negative thoughts will indeed take their toll on how we function. In contrast, the Alexander Technique speaks of the human condition in a much more positive way, in a way that celebrates our human abilities and gifts.

Alexander lessons enable us to experience the fact that evolution did not fall short of excellence when creating the human form. We are a success as bipeds. It is our evolutionary heritage to be elegantly vertical, and to maintain that verticality with ease and enjoyment. The truth of this can be experienced immediately in a lesson as we guide our students into moving with the head leading and the back following. And what about that demon, gravity? We evolved within a gravitational field. The Technique teaches us to release our muscles consciously so they can respond more efficiently to the gentle tug of gravity. This gentle tug helps maintain the normal supportive tone in our muscles and keeps them strong.

Another bit of good news I enjoy telling my students is that the harder they work at the Technique, the worse they will do. F.M. Alexander is quoted as saying that the biggest obstacle to doing well in a lesson is the desire to do well. "So," I tell my students, "the learning that occurs during a lesson is a very different experience from the learning you became used to in school. Here, you are to enjoy the process and not worry about the results." I tell them to let the Alexander thoughts float above their eyebrows and let their elegant nervous system take care of carrying the messages throughout the body. Occasionally a student will express disbelief that "just a thought" is powerful enough to cause a significant change in the state and functioning of the body. If thought can create tension headaches and other painful conditions, so can it be used to help the body heal and relieve pain.

One way I maintain contact with my colleagues in the world of physical therapy is by giving workshops on the Alexander Technique to other physical therapists. Most workshops taken by physical therapists are for the purpose of teaching therapeutic techniques that will benefit the patients the physical therapists will be treating. An Alexander workshop, however, is for the benefit of the physical therapists attending the workshop. They learn, through receiving a lot of Alexander hands-on experience, that they can make beneficial choices regarding their own use, and therefore take care of themselves while treating their patients. Another benefit physical therapists can achieve by applying the Alexander Technique to themselves as they work is to increase the sensitivity and effectiveness of their touch. As their own use improves, their hands become more sensitive, and they can receive clearer and more accurate information concerning the state and needs of their patients.

My belief in the benefit of exercising may have come from

my dance background as well as from my physical therapy work. The body stays healthier when it is regularly limbered and strengthened, as well as aerobically challenged. As all Alexander teachers know, however, there is an inherent danger in doing repetitive exercises: Unless taught otherwise, students will approach exercising with their habitual, harmful use. My solution is to eliminate the harmful use, not the exercising.

My most frequent problem with students who receive exercise programs elsewhere is to get them to do the exercises with less tension. I also find that they need to be guided into being aware of their entire body while exercising a specific area. For example, when doing an exercise to stretch their hamstring muscles, they would often have a lot of unnecessary tension in their neck and shoulders. Applying the Alexander principles to exercising eliminates this misuse and leads to efficiency and ease of movement. The benefits derived from exercising are then greatly enhanced.

I will approach a postural problem such as lordosis or round shoulders by drawing on both my professional areas. Physical therapy exercises are helpful in reducing these problems, but only if the faulty habits of use that caused them in the first place are changed by applying the Alexander Technique to daily life.

What is the best approach for treating a neck problem, such

as a herniated cervical disc, pinched nerves, severe arthritis or a whiplash injury? Evolution's great accomplishment of balancing the head (a large and heavy globe) on the top of the most flexible part of the spine deserves special consideration when it comes to treatment. I do not believe in giving strengthening exercises to the neck for these problems because most of the time such exercises just increase muscle tension and pain. Good use is, in itself, the best form of exercise for this area. As we go about doing our daily activities, we are automatically exercising the neck muscles in the best way possible if we are allowing the head to go forward and up instead of pulling it back and down. Allowing the head to be poised in a forward-up relation to the spine reduces pressure on nerves, discs, and sore joints, and facilitates the body healing itself.

As my students recover from a back injury, I encourage them to return to playing a sport, such as tennis or golf, that they enjoyed but had to stop because of the injury. The Alexander Technique is particularly helpful at this point. Alexander's directions of head leading and torso lengthening and widening will result in the abdominal and back muscles giving better support. An activity that may have been causing injury will now actually result in beneficially strengthening the body.

My physical therapy training has given me a lot of useful

information. There is no question in my mind that being familiar with the functioning of the musculoskeletal and neuromuscular systems is helpful in my Alexander work. However, I do not believe that this kind of information automatically makes me a better Alexander teacher. So how is it useful? Some students find it decreases their anxiety about their condition if they are given technical information and explanations. They will ask questions about nerve pathways, body mechanics, the structures of the spine, etc. My access to this information can be helpful for such patients.

I regard as one of the most valuable results of my physical therapy background the ability to describe Alexander's work to other medical people in terms they will find familiar. I can illustrate the power of a thought by quoting from J. V. Basmajian's textbook on electromyography, *Muscles Alive*, specifically from his chapter titled "Conscious Control and Training of Motor Units and Motor Neurons." In this chapter Basmajian describes studies that demonstrate the exquisite control we can develop over the nerve pathways that go to our skeletal muscles. We can learn to tell these pathways to be active or to rest in tranquil silence, and we can vary the rate and rhythm of their activity. Such skilled control is certainly part of "man's supreme inheritance." And I can remind those who know the nervous system well that inhibition is one of the most important functions of the higher centers of the nervous system, and that the Alexander Technique brings this vital function to the conscious level where it can be used to aid healing.

Today, Alexander teachers are seeking more technical knowledge about the body, and physical therapists are augmenting their healing skills with knowledge of approaches like the Alexander Technique. We have much to share that will enrich each other.

Every now and then one of my Alexander students will make a comment during a lesson that renews my sense of wonder about the Technique. These comments are of the type all teachers hear with regular frequency: "This work is so gentle and subtle, but so much is happening" or, "I don't feel as though I am doing anything and yet my whole world is changing." Even though I have been teaching Alexander's work over a span of 40 years, deep down inside me I am still amazed by the fact that the Alexander Technique "works." What is it that works? What is it that happens in a lesson?

When I first started teaching on my own, such questions were foremost in my mind, doubtless due to my inexperience and desire to do well. Now, however, I have had lots of experience, and am somewhat better at inhibiting my desire to do well while giving a lesson. Even so, I still have days when I wonder,

"What brings my students here? What makes them light up and leave my teaching room in a state of happiness and well-being?"

I still do not know all the answers to these questions. In my writings and lectures on Alexander's work I always try to be clear and non-mysterious. I am quite good at illustrating and explaining Alexander's genius in terms of human structure and function. But I realize that anatomy and neurology textbooks are about the human race as we know it now, whereas the Alexander Technique is about the human potential, the still-to-be-discovered. As a teacher, therefore, it is essential that I maintain my own state of alert awareness and non-doing so as not to limit the journey of each student. Each lesson I give has an unknown beginning and an unpredictable conclusion. Each student presents a unique self and each lesson is a unique adventure.

Before You Leap

❧ *by Anne Bluethenthal*

Movement never lies. . . . Dance should illuminate the landscape of the soul." As Martha Graham said, everything is there in a dancer's movement: her thoughts, feelings, dreams, and doubts. Her entire life history is expressed when she moves. Patterns and groupings on a stage, the architectural design of bodies, phrasing, and movement invention are all essential ingredients in the choreographic process. However, the vehicle of communication for this process is always the dancer.

Dance is the language of the soul spoken through movement. In the absence of words, a simple and mysterious communication is possible. Dance is movement poetry which the audience receives visually and feels in their body.

A dancer trains for years to become versed in this language by becoming strong, agile, and accomplished. She engages in a rigorous discipline to improve coordination and articulation. Her warm-ups are designed to build strength and range of movement, and her goal is to perform the most difficult movements with ease, grace, and passion.

As her training progresses, a simultaneous process is under way that will both direct and limit her future development. She is cultivating habits during her training that are, in large part, unintended and have great physical and psychic impact. In addition, these habits are being conveyed to the audience through her movement, thus altering the nature and meaning of her communication.

Imagine an actor who wants to convey anxiety without words. She will deliberately become more rigid and may move quickly and abruptly. Conversely, a dancer who is habitually rigid in the chest and shoulders, and who is generally tense, unwittingly will convey similar anxiety to the audience either visually or viscerally.

To plumb the depths of the soul, we need to make conscious the habits we cultivate in and out of the studio. If we inquire into our daily warm-up—the foundation for our dance training—we can ask what these exercises are inviting. Are they encouraging the building of brute strength, isolation of one body part from another, static positions, and the defiance of gravity? Or do they facilitate integration of the whole body through breathing, suppleness of muscular tone, minimizing of effort, and the use of gravity and momentum?

Each particular regimen represents a point of view. For example, what belief do I cultivate when I stand on a leg that is hardened at the thigh, clenched in the buttock, and tightened at the ankle with toes grabbing the floor for support? What values do I encourage by leaving the ankle free, letting the sole of the foot remain open with long toes, allowing the legs to be unbraced and leaving the hip joint mobile and the pelvic floor soft and open?

The point is you are creating your own instrument as you dance and train. What do you want that instrument to look like? What do you want it to be able to do? How will the type of practice you choose shape your instrument—your tool of expression?

As a young dancer, I trained in a variety of dance techniques in which I unconsciously cultivated attitudes and habits that later impeded my progress and, in some cases, led to injury. These attitudes, such as striving, fighting to get it right, and pushing through pain flow from our western urban culture.

Some of the neuromuscular patterns that accompany these mental states involve bracing in various muscle groups, raising the chest, holding on in the thighs and ankles, restricting the breathing, stiffening in the neck, and clenching in the gut.

In my early twenties, I had achieved a degree of mastery as a dancer, but I sensed I was nearing a ceiling in regard to my technical abilities. My body, while toned and strong, was also tight, uncomfortable, and continually plagued with knots, aches, and pains. This is not at all unusual. In fact, most dancers take pain for granted. We think that a rigorous workout is evidenced by the discomfort or pain that emerges later. Nevertheless, it started to dawn on me that these continual signs of strain might be unnecessary, if not harmful.

I also sensed some philosophical dissonance between the values I held in my intellectual and political life and the attitudes I was cultivating toward my inner self. I considered myself an ardent feminist. At the heart of my feminism was a belief in integration rather than divisiveness, both within a person and among people. Yet, in the studio I was trying to force my body with a tyrannical tone into appropriate positions, cultivating an aggressive, competitive attitude toward myself.

As Erick Hawkins (a choreographer and dancer whose maverick approach to modern dance derives from the science of kinesiology and a philosophy of simplicity, purity, and non-doing) said, "The way of tight muscles, tension, strain, violence, force and aggressiveness in the body, registers the analogous state of the soul."

While in college, I had the good fortune to fall into the hands of a teacher who was a Sufi and a former dancer with the Erick Hawkins Dance Company. She embodied an aesthetic I had never imagined. She performed extraordinary technical movements with a beautiful quality of grace and ease. It was clear that she was genuinely at ease while executing even the most strenuous movements.

Under her instruction, I totally reconfigured my understanding of my own body as well as my approach to dance training. I acquired practical experience with the principle of non-doing in an activity. I discovered that when I was engaged in the most athletic feat, there could be, in my core, a still, calm place from which the movement could emanate. When such an open, quiet center was operating, I was more awake and able to observe as I moved. Furthermore, I was able to determine the effort that was actually necessary to accomplish the movement.

For the first time, I realized that the effort I was putting into my dancing was the main impediment to my improvement. Through this new insight, a flood of changes ensued. I learned how to work on my dancing by a process that required less effort, which meant I had a lot more energy at my disposal. In addition, the less I did in a muscular way, the more I felt; in fact, it was as though with each "letting go" of habitual grabbing, there was an explosion of sensation. These changes affected my whole relationship with the floor. Gravity became something to work with and be supported by rather than to lift out of or defy. Instead of relying on fixed positions and holding, I started dancing with poise, flow and grace. Gradually my fear diminished while my sense of confidence and vulnerability grew. I began to feel that I was no longer making dance happen but allowing movement to flow through me.

As I was beginning to teach dance during this time, I had a question for my teacher about how to approach a specific movement: "Should we be using our abdominals as we curve the torso forward in the sitting warm-up or just let the body fall and recover itself?" Her reply: "That depends on what is important to you in life." Her answer, simple as it seemed, shattered my preconceptions about teaching and learning dance technique. She helped me realize that the values I hold dear in my life are the same ones that shape my training. In fact, they act on each other reciprocally. All the minute choices we make, can and do shape our beliefs. They are not themselves fixed, but become part of a process of discovery.

This sense of dance training as a process of discovery will emerge once we are able to observe the choices we are making—even the subtle ones that affect the amount of muscular effort made. Then we can begin to question, investigate and consciously guide our own training. For example, I may ask: Can I do this movement with less constriction of breath? With less grabbing in my muscles? What do I wish to communicate? Can I display aggression or power without harming myself? What impact will holding my abdominals for several hours a day have on my physical and mental well being? Is there a way of achieving technical excellence through less effort?

Over time, however, I found that even a technique of less effort and sounder kinesiological principles was not sufficient. My dancing was still limited by the deep neuromuscular patterns and unconscious habits that underlay all of my activities in and out of the studio.

As dancers train and develop—perhaps this is true in other activities as well, but I find it particularly true of dance—it is very easy to become dependent on guidance from the outside. We rely on the teacher and the mirror to determine success, correctness, and degree of progress. We are not taught to observe our internal sensory activities. Consequently, we are surprised to find the aches, pains, and moods that arise after rigorous work, and we may feel alarmed and puzzled by an injury of unknown origin.

In my investigation into these issues I came across the Alexander Technique, which has become the basis of my approach to movement, the body, teaching, and my understanding of the nature of habit and thought. The Technique is in essence a training in wakeful doing. That is, we learn to observe ourselves in stillness and carry that attention into activity. Additionally, from that base of stillness and attention, we learn to consciously direct our actions or movements not by doing but by holding an intention in mind. Attention with intention is the cornerstone of Alexander's work.

On a purely mechanical level it is easy to point out how habits interfere with carrying out an intention: An actor who is in the habit of constricting the throat muscles during speech will usually find his pitch rising when, in fact, he means to increase his volume. Consider the dancer who is in the habit of raising her shoulders during an effortful movement. If she attempts a double pirouette, she is likely to fall backwards as the increased effort to turn takes her off-balance—rather than taking her up and around her central axis.

To the extent that these are gross muscular distortions, any teacher can point out the visible movement error and ask for a correction. However, the typical suggestion involves doing: "Bring your shoulders down." Or, "Hold onto your alignment as you turn." One is not likely to hear, "Observe the clenching in your neck and shoulders at the moment you begin to move." Or, "See if you can refrain from raising the shoulders, and keep that intention to remain quiet in the shoulder girdle as you move." These requests would indicate both non-doing as a corrective tool and internal observation as a guiding principle.

After examining what one's training entails from a formal point of view, we can look at the internal process, i.e., the internal landscape you build along with your technical prowess. The direction of non-doing first involves the incorporation of an observing self in the practice of dance. Developing powers of observation requires a continual inquiry into the workings of the mind, the heart, and the body: What thoughts, feelings and sensations arise as a part of, and in dialogue with, your daily practice? What level of neuromuscular effort are you employing as you rehearse?

This approach guarantees that as a dancer continues her daily practice, she is strengthening not only her muscles, but her ability to observe in activity and to maintain equilibrium in the midst of dancing. When a movement is attempted that causes strain, she will likely notice it and be able to make a conscious choice regarding that strain. Self-observation also allows her increasing insight into her own behavior.

With non-doing, observation, and conscious intention as the basis for training and practice, underlying habits of thought and action are more accessible. We can observe the bracing and rigidity that cause unwanted responses or movements, or that limit our capacity for improvement. These patterns weaken the integrity of our organism, create the conditions for injury, and communicate to an audience our anxiety and disconnectedness.

I may discover that in the moment prior to a jump, I am bearing down in the chest and gut as a preparation. After examining this pattern, I'm likely to discover that not only is this bearing down unnecessary, it is actually counterproductive as I will certainly not get as much height as I would were I to leave the torso quiet and buoyant. In addition, this kind of preparing causes a tugging on the lower back which weakens the structure and often leads to muscle pulls and spasms. Of course, the other unwanted effect is that such a preparation telegraphs to an audience that something difficult is about to happen—the magic of leaping effortlessly is lost.

This approach to one's self and one's training requires a radical shift in attitude. Instead of seeing the body as a static set of conditions to be positioned, corrected, tamed, and polished, we become a continually changing process of events, responses, and choices that may be observed, quieted, redirected, or left alone.

The first rule of this approach to one's self and one's dancing is to stop fighting. In fact, it is to stop entirely. To observe, one first has to stop doing. Once the observing self is active, one's job is to remain attentive as one proceeds into activity.

Poise, integrity, and coordination will not be achieved by force. The body's integrity reveals itself when we refrain from interfering with that very balance. Our work is to observe how we interfere, and how we address ourselves in a tyrannical tone—dividing one part from another. We can then begin to learn a new kind of "control."

When a dancer cultivates this kind of attentiveness during training, the result is an artist who is not only more "awake," but also more conscious of how she is executing her movement and what she is communicating through it. The dancer is less limited by her unconscious habits and is therefore freer to say what she intends. Her movement reveals an inner landscape that is more essential, whole and universal. This movement speaks not from the personality of the dancer to that of the audience, but from the depth of one soul to another.

Meeting the Unexpected

❧ *by Mary Holland*

lthough I had Alexander lessons from an early age, I never really expected as a child that I would one day become a teacher of this work, or of anything else for that matter. My childhood dreams were of a more exotic nature. As children, my sisters and I were always either acting in our own plays, miming to Gilbert and Sullivan records (complete with costumes and complicated dance routines), or dressing up in our bedroom curtains and performing scenes from Shakespeare for our parents and their friends, and I imagined that life would continue in this delightful way!

But when, at 18, the time came for leaving school and deciding on further studies, for some reason I did not have the courage or confidence to pursue my dreams of the Theatre, or in fact even to tell anyone about them. They remained in the background, along with the idea that perhaps I didn't have enough talent, and the fear that I would not be good enough. At the time of course I didn't really appreciate how fortunate and unusual it was to be given lessons in the Alexander Technique. I had several from my father, Sydney Holland, who himself trained with Alexander, and others from John Skinner, Peggy Williams, Walter Carrington, and one from F.M. himself. Before I had even left school I did talk to Walter about possibly doing the Alexander training course—it is so long ago I can't really remember what my reasons were, but I do remember that with kindness and wisdom Walter told me that I was still a bit too young, and that in this world it is a good idea to have some kind of recognized qualification. This was very good advice, and so, encouraged by my Art teacher, I did a three year Art School training in graphic design. Then I worked for a few years in a small, lively advertising agency designing, among other things, boxes for dog biscuits, catalogues for a rather posh mail order fashion business and, I hate to admit it, cigarette packets!

The work was all very interesting and challenging, but I had a nagging feeling that I did not belong in that world, that I was meant to be doing something else. In my spare time, I had gained some good experience in a well-organized amateur theatre, the Questors in Ealing, and this eventually led me to do what I had originally wanted to do. Somehow I got some courage, did a few auditions, obtained a grant and finally made it to Drama School, where I spent two years learning about voice and movement, characterization, stage make up, script analysis and fencing. A contract with the Bristol Old Vic theatre followed, where I discovered what life in the theatre is really about—sheer hard work!

But what wonderful work. It was as though life had suddenly moved into another gear where everything was new and intense and exciting. But after a while—and this I really hadn't expected—the feeling came again that something was not quite right. I had achieved my dream, but I often was depressed and frustrated. My life was not as satisfying and fulfilling as I had hoped.

Then I found out that there were inevitable periods of being out of work. Difficult as it was, it did give me the opportunity to take time, to stop and think a bit. Often this act of stopping can allow space for the unexpected to happen. Fear of stopping, fear of quietness, fear of feeling how we really are can cause our inner and outer lives to follow fixed predictable paths. It took me a long time to realize what a trap fixed ideas and expectations are, and even longer to be able to identify some of mine, and so to begin the process of letting them go.

It was hard facing the fact that acting had not been everything that I had expected. I hated being out of work and feeling useless, and in time began to wonder whether I would now be ready to do the Alexander Training Course, if they would have me. At the age of 28 I had a bit more experience of living, and had some experience applying the Technique to the process of acting. I had found that, when I was capable of remembering, inhibition and direction could be invaluable tools in rehearsal and performance, giving me an idea of what it could be like to function in a freer way. Unfortunately these moments were sporadic and short-lived, and I hoped that if I did the training I would come to understand what was getting in my way. The practical problem of doing the training was that either I was working and had the money but no time, or I was out of work and had the time but no money! Walter did agree to take me on, and through a combination of luck, generosity and fortunate timing it became possible for me to devote the three years just to doing the training.

During this time I had many unexpected psycho-physical experiences, including dealing with long held and previously unconscious tensions, that were difficult to meet. Gradually it dawned on me that for most of my life I had been neither present nor awake, and consequently had been rather handicapped in meeting anything or anybody, let alone the unexpected. As a result of all the Alexander work I was receiving, I was able to stop stiffening my neck quite so much, I got a bit better at remembering to inhibit and direct, and surprise, surprise, I even began to allow myself to breathe! This led to glimpses of what it was like to be in a better state—and these moments always took me by surprise.

The first dramatic instance of this change came when I was walking down the street one day after class, and suddenly noticed that I felt, in every way, lighter and freer: almost happy. This interested me because my circumstances had not changed; I still had a situation in my private life that could make me unhappy, but somehow my reaction to the situation had changed. There seemed to be a developing possibility of choice, of choosing to make myself unhappy, or of choosing not to make myself unhappy.

Then one day in class, during my second year I think, Walter was helping me work on another student, and had his hands on my neck and shoulder. Suddenly something released in me, and I had the feeling that I was coming out of a thick fog! Everything was brighter and more defined, and I was aware of myself, my surroundings and the other people with a clarity that was new to me.

For many years I suffered from migraines, and lying on the table one day at school I felt the all too familiar signs—pressure on the right side of my head and around my right eye, stiff ankles, and uncontrollable disconnected thought—that another one was about to develop. Dilys Carrington came over and silently worked for a few minutes on my head and neck. She moved away and I realized with amazement that through this brief sensory experience my pattern of thinking had radically altered. My thoughts were more ordered and not so negative, and gradually the pressure diminished. It was invaluable to become aware that a situation that I had been sure could only go in one direction (that is to get worse to the point of almost unbearable pain accompanied by vomiting) had taken a different turn and had not developed in the usual way.

The process of becoming more aware is of course an ongoing one. How lovely it would be if one day we could say: "Now I've achieved it!" It isn't like that, and luckily alongside the awareness, one's reactions to that awareness undergo a change too. Recently, in connection to a visit to the cinema I was able to observe, identify and release some interesting patterns of fixation. And of course fixed ideas and expectations are inextricably bound up with physical tensions and fixations. You don't get one without the other. On this occasion my first realization was that I had prejudged the film, and was preparing myself for two hours of boredom to please a friend. So I stopped doing that and tried to be more open to the unexpected. Then I got furious when we were given tickets in the third row. Oh no, I thought, I can't face having to sit the whole time looking uncomfortably up at the screen. And when I found out that in that small cinema there were in fact only six rows, so that actually we would be sitting in the middle, and that the film turned out to be rather good, I had to laugh at myself for nearly ruining the evening with my habitual nonsense!

Soon after I qualified from the training course I kept my connection to the theatre by working in a couple of Drama Schools, and slowly my own wish or need to act faded into the background. In my new career I struggled for a while with the labels 'teacher' and 'Technique.' What do I mean, "for a while?" I'm still struggling with the meanings of these words. The former seems liable to evoke all kinds of expectations in both 'teacher' and 'pupil,' and the latter, contrary to my experience of the work as life-giving and positive, sounds a bit rigid and clinical. Working with private pupils was sometimes impossibly difficult, especially as I still suffered from occasional appalling migraines, but then came the joyful discovery that however insecure, inadequate and inept I feel, "it works" and people really do benefit and change (all through non-doing)—and sometimes quite dramatically.

When it comes to dramatic change, perhaps the most unexpected thing I ever did was leave England after 17 years of working at Walter and Dilys Carrington's Constructive Teaching Centre and come to teach in Munich, Germany. The opportunity came about through a series of meetings and coincidences that were too extraordinary to ignore. It started with the secretary at the Centre asking me if I would be willing to give some lessons to a German lady who would be in London over Christmas. If I had not said "yes" then, I probably would not be here in Germany now. Actually the lady turned out to be a delightful American living in Munich, who liked the Alexander Technique so much that she sent her singing teacher, who in turn sent two of her students. One of them sent a theatre director, and so over a few months I built up a few contacts in Munich.

It struck me at the time that these pupils visiting from abroad made very rapid positive changes. It could have been because they were away from their habitual environment, they had time for themselves, and most of them took daily lessons for a period of two or three weeks. Obviously no one can afford to do that very often, so these visits had come to an end, when a year or two later, through an unrelated referral I started to give lessons to another German pupil. During one of his lessons, just for something to say really, I asked him where he was from in Germany. A normal enough question, but something strange happened to my awareness of time. In what must have been a very brief moment between my question and his reply, I had the feeling that time had somehow expanded and that much more was available to me. And in this time somehow before he said anything I knew that he was going to say "Munich," and I also knew, without really knowing why, that one day I would go there.

It was almost as though that expanded experience of time gave me the space to discern a new direction—a direction that had certainly never occurred to me before. Germany? Munich? Why?

A week later during one of this student's lessons, there was a phone call from someone in Munich who had just heard about the Technique and wanted to know if there were any teachers there. This seemed a strange coincidence, to which my pupil responded by suggesting that I should visit, adding that he could find me pupils and somewhere to teach. During 1983 I visited a few times, and it was marvelous to be met at the airport, driven to town, taken out to lunch and over coffee be handed my timetable of eight lessons a day for the next two or three weeks! Then I found that dividing myself between two places was not good for anybody, not for the pupils in London or Munich who didn't get enough continuous work, and certainly not for me because I was always exhausted. So I realized I would have to make a choice.

During the time it took to come to my decision I found that I needed a lot of time quietly on my own at home, doing nothing, just waiting. Sometimes I would do 15 minutes of whispered ahs because they helped clear my mind. And when my mind had cleared a bit, I was able to let go of the fixed idea that I didn't have the strength for such a move, and it gradually became clear to me that whether I liked it or not, the direction I had to go was over the Channel and down to Munich. I rented out my flat in London, said good-bye to everyone and jumped into the unknown.

Living in a foreign country brings one face to face with the unexpected at every moment. A completely new environment can be quite an overwhelming sensory experience. And Munich is a beautiful city. There are historic churches, grand old apartment buildings, open air food markets, new office blocks, parks and beer gardens, and busy streets, where trams still run. The mingled smells of mulled wine and roasted almonds in the Christmas market were quite wonderful. And all the time one is hearing new noises, how the telephone rings for example, as well as the endless sounds and rhythms of a new language. There is nothing like learning a new language later in life to help shake up old patterns of thought. It is just not possible to think in your habitual way when trying to express yourself with new words and structures.

The newness of the environment wasn't the only disturbance to my system. Setting up as the only Alexander teacher living in Munich brought me fairly soon up against an unforeseen horror. A Naturopath pupil of mine sent me one of his patients with a back problem, unfortunately telling this man that I was the only person who could help him. He came for a few lessons, and instead of getting the instant positive result he expected, he felt the return of an old pain, which upset him so much that he lodged a complaint against me. This complaint resulted in my having to be interviewed by a doctor in the Ministry of Health. To explain the work we do to someone with no experience of it is a hard enough challenge in our native language, and in my almost non-existent German I knew it would be impossible, so I took a friend along to help. The interview went quite well, and there would have been no further action, except for the fact that my pupil was determined to press charges, and some weeks later I received a letter summoning me to an interview with the Criminal Police, and accusing me—incredibly enough—of illegally practicing medicine.

When this interview finally took place, my lawyer and a doctor friend came with me. The session began with a young policeman taking details of my name and address and date of birth, and I remember that he did have a slight twinkle in his eye when he asked me the final question, which was, "And what previous crimes have you committed?" It was all much easier than I had expected. The man who had accused me didn't even bother to turn up, but instead sent a letter to inform us that his back was getting better. I seem to remember that the policemen, lawyer and doctor spent most of the time not bothering about me but chatting and laughing with each other. This suited me fine. Also the doctor who had interviewed me in the Ministry of Health had written to confirm that the work I did was teaching and not pretending to be medical treatment. The case was eventually thrown out, and a potentially dangerous situation, not only for me, but for the whole profession, was defused.

During the nine months that this situation took to resolve itself I had plenty of opportunity to observe how I was dealing with so much stress. Not always well! My psycho-physical state swung between feelings of guilt, shame and embarrassment, accompanied by dreadful imaginings of the worst that could happen—condemnation and/or banning of the Technique in Germany, deportation or even prison—contrasted by an occasional sense of complete calmness and an inner conviction that somehow I was being looked after, and that everything would turn out all right. All this time I had wonderful support from pupils and friends, which I needed, because it wasn't until it was all over that I dared to mention it to anyone in England.

A few years later, in a bizarre accident, I got shaken up even more. Early one morning in my studio, while waiting for my students to come, I slipped and fell, hitting the back of my head with a loud crack on the wooden edge of my teaching chair. At first I didn't think it was too bad, but as the day wore on I felt more and more weird, and as I lay in bed that night my whole brain and spine gradually got hotter and hotter to the point of seeming to be on fire. I felt in danger, alone and helpless, being incapable even of calling for assistance. Every now and again I looked at the clock noting that another hour or so had passed, and that to my surprise I was still alive. Strangely enough I don't recall being frightened. I survived the night, and when I got to see a doctor, she diagnosed concussion. The German word literally translates as "shaking of the brains," which is a very good description of what it felt like. Because I nearly fainted in her office she called an ambulance and they took me straight to the hospital and x-rayed my head. They said nothing was broken but that they would keep me there, as complete rest and quiet were necessary. Something told me that a hospital is not the ideal place for peace and quiet, so I came home instead, where a few friends looked after me, bringing me food and drink and treating me with a kindness, thoughtfulness and generosity that I will never forget.

For two weeks I just lay in bed. I couldn't move, I couldn't read, I couldn't listen to music, light bothered me, sound bothered me, and I couldn't even bear anyone near me for more than a few minutes—and the sound of a voice seemed to get right inside my head and disturb my brain. The simplest movement—turning over in bed, for example—even when slowly and carefully performed, caused an increase in the unpleasant sensation of fullness and fuzziness in my head. So when possible I chose not to move, not even to think, especially negative thoughts, because they quite literally hurt my brain. Later I monitored my progress by my ability to tolerate sound. At first, I could only listen to one instrument playing something slowly. A quickening of pace, or more instruments joining in was immediately distressing. Eventually, listening to a quartet was a big achievement. It took me nearly two years to be able to watch a film without getting dizzy, and even longer to be able to drink alcohol without my brain complaining.

Gradually coming out of this state was a little like being reborn. It was a slow process. The first stage was accepting the state that I was in, acknowledging that I was hurt and fairly helpless and weak, and not trying to deny or fight against it. This led to experiencing a deep sense of peace and quietness.

Then, out of this quietness, I had to learn to function again. When I could get out of bed, one of the first movements that I worked with was kneeling on the floor, then sitting back on my heels, followed by allowing my head to lead me slowly forward from the hips to rest my hands on the floor. This position felt safe and comforting, and the procedure when repeated gradually built up my awareness of my back again, and with it the sense that I had a bit of strength and support. With no sense of my back I felt less integrated and whole. So allowing it to come back into my consciousness was very important for my recovery and healing. And of course my whole muscular system was weakened from lying in bed, but gradually doing some work with crawling and walking brought things to life again. Movement was only possible, however, with lots of inhibition and direction—I could really feel how thoughtless uncoordinated movement, like the negative thoughts, caused distress to my whole system.

Years ago I read a story of an old Chinese farmer who to everything that happened to him, from the seemingly tragic to the surprisingly fortunate, commented only, "Who knows what is good and what is bad?" I think he is right: Often we don't know. The experiences that I have just related, apparently so difficult and unpleasant, have in fact enriched me beyond measure.

And since taking my plunge into the unknown many more obviously delightful unexpected happenings have come my way. From each one of the many remarkable people that I have met I have learned a great deal. Four years ago I did a clown course, and learned how a clown has no expectations whatsoever, and sees everything as if for the first time. Our first exercise was to stand alone on stage, put on a red nose—and do nothing. Not to plan, not to try to be funny, in other words just to inhibit, and wait and see what happened to you standing there with twelve strangers looking at you. Perhaps that is why I had to come to Germany—to put on a red nose!

And recently, quite out of the blue, I have had the chance to act again in a small theatre that sometimes puts on plays in English here. What is even more amazing is that it was the role of a lifetime in an outstanding play. I had the great good fortune to play Paulina Salas in Ariel Dorfmans' *Death and the Maiden*. It was something I just had to do, the right part at the right moment, giving me an opportunity to explore and express pain and anger and power.

And in this process the Technique was a tremendous help. It was easier now to inhibit the desire to perform well or to impress. I could let go a bit the habit of trying and forcing, and found it easier to keep in mind the overall flow and direction of the scene and play. Interestingly enough there was hardly a glimmer of my old fear that I would not be good enough. But perhaps most importantly I was able sometimes to dare to take time and wait and see what happened unexpectedly on its own, without my doing anything. And I noticed that my improved sensory awareness allowed me right from the very first reading to feel a better connection to myself, the text, and the other actors than I had felt previously even after weeks of rehearsal. My sister, who came over from England to see the show, said it was as though I had finally discovered what I really enjoyed doing—strutting around the stage with a gun, tying someone up with my tights, gagging them with my knickers, and swearing like a trooper!

But, seriously, the role was demanding, it was harrowing, and it was exhilarating. It was as though a circle had been completed, because at last being on stage, performing, and really being there, was, unexpectedly, the totally inspiring and fulfilling experience that I had longed for all those years ago.

Who knows what will happen next? None of us do, of course. Maybe all we can do is work on being ready to meet whatever the next moment may bring with as much poise and balance as are available to us. Often the most wonderful things happen when we least expect them, so if we don't want to miss them we had better be ready!

The Actor's Consciousness and the Character's Consciousness

❧ by Phyllis G. Richmond

I have been involved with theater as a teacher, director, movement coach, and performer. For the past several years I have been teaching the Alexander Technique to actors studying in a Stanislavski-based professional actor training program at Southern Methodist University. The more I work with actors, the more I realize how closely the Alexander Technique supports a Stanislavski-based approach to acting. I believe these two approaches in combination make a significant contribution to contemporary actor training.

Acting is a unique creative process. An actor on stage is really two people at once: the actor and the character, each with a unique role to play in making the performance happen. The character's consciousness is inside the play—the character is the one to whom the play is reality, the one who feels the emotions, has the intentions, executes the actions. The actor's consciousness monitors the process of bringing the character to life, to make sure the actor speaks loudly enough, finds the hot spot, registers laughter and waits for it to subside, adjusts blocking to compensate for a scene partner in the wrong place, checks for and releases unnecessary tension, and so forth. The actor's consciousness facilitates the character's consciousness, attending to the conditions that allow the actor to go about the work of playing the character and proceeding through the journey of the play.

Performing involves juggling many different and demanding stimuli at once. The actor needs to be able to attend to both internal and external stimuli at the same moment, to be aware of actor, character, fellow performers, the particular moment in the play, and the audience at the same time. The actor must be seen, heard, and understood throughout the theater, must keep a certain pace and blocking, and must take the same actions essentially the same way every night. And each performance must be as if for the first time, newly minted, spontaneous, easy and natural.

This is the paradox: the demands of the external and internal realities may not be the same—the actor may be playing an intimate moment of self-revelation that must be heard in the back of the balcony. The actor needs to find a way to integrate the external technical realities of being on stage with the internal emotional realities of the specific role.

The connection between inner and outer aspects of acting technique must be developed so that it becomes second nature to express inner reality in outer form. Konstantin Stanislavski, the great Russian director and acting teacher, whose work is the foundation for the "Method" (the dominant acting tradition in the United States) speaks of the general creative state, a state of inner and outer coordination:

"When you are in this state every feeling, every mood that wells up inside you is reflexively expressed....all your inner resources and physical capacities are on call, ready to respond to any bid....The more immediate, spontaneous, vivid, precise the reflection you produce from inner to outer form, the better, broader, fuller will be your public's sense of the inner life of the character you are portraying on the stage...." (Stanislavski, *Building a Character*, p. 274).

Actor training is, in part, learning psychological techniques of analysis, intuition, and imagination, as well as physical techniques of vocal production, speech and movement. The challenge is to learn these techniques so well that they are fully integrated into the actor's way of being and therefore are invisible as techniques in performance. The audience should not be aware of the techniques, but only of the performance. The problem is that the act of performing creates tension that can interfere with performance.

"In ordinary life you walk and sit and talk and look but on the stage you lose these faculties. You feel the closeness of the public and you say to yourself, 'Why are they looking at me?'...All our acts become strained...before a public of a thousand people." (Stanislavski, *An Actor Prepares*, p. 71,73)

The actor may ask: What needs to happen next? Where do I need to be? How must I react? How must I feel? How can I get from where I am to where I need to be emotionally in the next scene? Is the audience with me? Too often, the actor will rely on effort to manipulate dramatic action instead of relying on preparation and process. He may think he needs to feel effort, sweat and strain to know that he is working. He may develop habits that comfort him into feeling he is doing something right. He may get locked into formulae of playing each beat/scene/line so that he is sure of what is happening. By trying to force emotion to happen in a certain way, the actor creates tension that lodges in the musculature and actually blocks emotion.

Experience does not forge feelings to order—feelings happen

by themselves. When the actor's process works well, the intention leads to action through the imagination alone. The actors really listen to each other, hear each other, respond to each other, and the play goes from line to line, from action to action, from beat to beat, from scene to scene with clarity and irrefutable inner logic. However, self-created physical tension gets in the way of playful responsiveness and blocks the path of creative expression.

For many actors, the familiar responses to stimuli naturally produced under normal conditions disappear under the abnormal conditions of being on stage. The actor feels stressed by the pressure to perform and then needs to deal with the stress in order to perform. Stress has two components: the stressor and the individual's response to the stressor. The actor cannot change the stressor, the special characteristics of the theatrical situation: sets, costumes, makeup, blocking, lines, fellow actors, audience. But the actor can manage his response to these factors. Actual physical and physiological changes occur in response to stress, generating a heightened physical and mental state. A heightened state in response to performance is normal and desirable, for it improves performance. But sometimes the changes are not so welcome, as when muscular tension causes gripping in the back, raising of the shoulders, stiffening the limbs, bracing the chest, tightening the neck, and related physiological changes such as uncontrollably racing heartbeat, shaking, temperature fluctuations. These are not the responses of the character but of the actor, and the actor needs to use all his skill not to let this heightened state of tension interfere with the behavior of the character. The actor needs to monitor and eliminate self-created tension in order to prevent interference with the creative process. This is where the Alexander Technique can play a vital function by helping the actor manage his or her self-created tension.

Stanislavski warned that muscular tension has disastrous effects on the creative state—and yet recognized that the actor may not be able to prevent tension. "Let the tenseness come...if you cannot avoid it. But immediately let your control step in and remove it," he wrote (Stanislavski, *An Actor Prepares*, p. 94). Stanislavksi called the monitor of tension the "controller." While the word "controller" may have negative connotations of tension and emotional repression for a modern audience, Stanislavksi was referring to giving up tension, emotional repression, and manipulative control.

In the Alexander Technique the "controller" is the process of Inhibition and Direction: awareness of what is happening in the body, prevention of inappropriate automatic habits of use, redirection of the neuromuscular system to organize good use that supports poise, coordination, freedom, and openness to the moment. Engaging in this process, it is possible to maintain perspective on what is happening and not to become unduly anxious or tense. It is possible to allow anxiety to run its course without panic, to guard against undue tension, and to continue to focus on the acting process. The ability to take command empowers the actor to choose to become vulnerable. When the actor stops creating unnecessary tension that blocks feeling, then feeling may well up of its own accord to seek external expression. When the actor is open to what is going on within her, then she also will be open to her scene partner, ready to listen and respond, free to make choices, execute actions and let the passion play through her. The actor is by definition in the moment when she is aware of what is happening in the moment. She is neither caught up in judging what just happened nor in the throes of anticipating what will happen next.

It is a risk to give oneself permission not to force but to allow response, to be present and to trust in imagination and preparation. Even when the actor believes that this is the way to proceed, the pressure to produce a performance sometimes makes it difficult to take this path. Being open and vulnerable can feel downright scary, for if you let go of control, you cannot be sure what will happen. When the actor learns to inhibit physical tension and mental manipulation, something different than the usual result will happen. If you stop doing A, then B, C, D or E can happen. If you stop constricting the throat, the voice comes out. If you stop suppressing the emotions through tension and then forcing the display of emotion, emotion can happen of its own accord.

It has been my experience teaching the Alexander Technique to actors that when the self-created tension is eliminated the performance improves. The actor finds the process less effortful both mentally and physically, and the performance flows more easily. Marissa Catubig, actress and SMU graduate, experienced this change in her work when, instead of struggling with the unintentional repression of emotion through tension, she let full-blooded emotion out freely:

"I often felt my neck tensing, my face thickening, my hands very tense with emotion...and my mind was a blank because I was so focused on "feeling" instead of doing, just releasing and letting it happen. For the past couple of weeks...I've been acting without creating tension and when it works it actually works. It's amazing. I mean, I can still have emotions, but I don't have to pop my blood vessels and stop breathing to let them emerge."

When she stopped interfering with the acting and then overcoming the interference in order to act, she saved herself a lot of extra work. The process became simpler and easier. The actor's consciousness can undo the self-created interference, leaving a living, breathing core of receptivity and readiness around which to build a performance. Stanislavski warns against the same syndrome of forcing feeling.

"Do not force or do violence to your feelings if your soul does not catch fire....Make this a rule: The more dramatically powerful a scene is, the greater the call on your inner forces, the freer your body must be....watch your hands with especial care: no clenched fists, no twisting of fingers. If you ball your fists you are done for because you will have shut in your temperament, driven it deep inside." (Stanislavski, *Stanislavski on Opera*, p. 36)

The actor must command the most intelligent use possible within the context of the requirements of the production to meet the physical and mental challenge of the character in a way that is not ultimately damaging to the actor. As the challenges increase, as the pressure rises in rehearsal and performance, the tendency to tense up is greater. It is important to prevent this cycle if the actor expects to perform well repeatedly over time. In moments of high emotion on stage it is particularly important to work within a released instrument. The actor needs to take care of himself continuously while remaining fully engaged, to be conscious on two levels at once, as performer and as character, in order to tend to both sets of needs. John Harrell, an actor and an MFA graduate of SMU, faced this challenge playing Orgon in a very physical production of *Tartuffe*.

"The rage was an important part of the character, lashing out against a world that just wouldn't listen to him or take him seriously. However, I out of necessity had to construct a physical shell that was as relaxed as possible and yet still read rage to the audience. If I allowed the emotion to create the posture by itself, it ripped apart my back....Many times I would sense that my body temperature was far too high and therefore I must be working extremely hard—too hard....I learned to have the actor's thought process while using the Alexander process to inhibit and then make the best possible choice in the moment....I gave myself permission to say yes to relaxation on stage while continuing to work within the moment." Harrell discovered that by engaging in the Alexander process of preventing unnecessary tensions and organizing himself in a free and open way he was able to take care of himself as an actor while remaining fully involved in the performance, respecting his needs both as artist and human being.

Ideally, good use of oneself is ultimately not noticed as such by the audience. In fact it should not be noticed at all—the performance should be noticed, not what the actor is doing to perform. Sometimes the demands of a role and the overt appearance of good use dovetail harmoniously. The actor may need to be physically neutral, well-aligned and well-coordinated with appropriate self-organization which does not draw undue attention. However, good use does not necessarily mean looking as if you have good posture. The role might call for slouching or collapsing or severe physical distortions. The actor may be asked to transform physically to inhabit another body with alien physical characteristics: a swayback, a hump, a limp, arthritis, paralysis, a hangover....In order to be able to play a character with potentially disabling misuse it is crucial to replace muscle tension with mental attention to organize the appropriate coordination.

Each actor has a personal method for working out physical characterization through some combination of intuition, analysis, exploration and conscious choice to determine what is possible and necessary, what feels and looks right, and how it can be done. The Alexander concept of *use* can provide a key to the character's body. How does this character hold his spine? What is his postural behavior? How does he pose his head? How does he carry his weight? How does he coordinate his limbs? How does he feel about his body? Keeping in mind that the character does not want to be uncomfortable and is doing the best she or he can under the circumstances, I as actor do not want to create unnecessary tension. I can alter my self-organization to explore how the character organizes posture and movement. But I do not want to go so far into misuse that it hurts or incapacitates me. I can utilize what I know to discover how expanded and connected I can be within that body, not forcing the character's posture but allowing my body to settle in with a regard for my well-being. I can utilize my consciousness of use to explore how to inhabit a tense body without making myself unduly tense. It is not necessary or useful for me to tie myself into knots, nor is it necessary for me to be destructively tense for the audience to get the message of tension. I may slouch, but I lengthen and widen within that slouch, so that I am as open and expanded as possible within the physical constraints set by the choice of physical characterization. The challenge is to perform the appearance of misuse repeatedly over time without harm and without getting stuck in the reality of misuse.

I coached a production of *One flew Over the Cuckoo's Nest* at SMU which required many cast members to wrestle with this problem. The inmates of the asylum in *One Flew Over the Cuckoo's Nest* manifested their unique psychological disturbances through idiosyncratic patterns of misuse and distortion. One actor chose to be almost doubled over, tailbone tucked under, chest collapsed, head poking forward, eyes intensely open, hallucinating. This could have become a frozen posture causing stiffness, backache, sore neck. By lengthening, widening and releasing within these choices, the actor could continue to breathe and not stiffen—and walk away after performance without any pain. The challenge in such a situation is to allow the disturbed posture and movement to happen from a core of lengthening and expansion, so the actor does not go into spasm or become fixed in this unpleasant condition. To succeed in this, I suggested the actor move consciously into the appearance of misuse from his own best use, explore the nature of misuse, and later consciously move out of misuse into neutral. In other words, the Alexander Technique can provide a place to begin and end physical characterization.

I learned about the importance of consciously leaving the character and becoming myself again while rehearsing and performing in Beckett's *Act Without Words II*. I was playing character A who is so involved with his own discomfort and angst that he is not fully aware of the outside world. I got stuck inside that inner-turned, irritable, collapsed, fuzzy-headed, physically painful, muddled, negative, complaining, brooding, depressed state. One evening I went out onto the streets of New York not paying any attention to what I was doing and got on the wrong subway. Suddenly, I snapped awake, frightened because I did not know where I was. I realized that I had been completely oblivious to my surroundings. I understood how critical it is to be sure you come back to yourself after rehearsal or performance. I can do that through consciously coming out of the character's body, back to my own body. The actor's consciousness must facilitate the character's consciousness, not merge with it. It is important for me as actor to stay with myself, no matter how involved I am with the character.

Consciously monitoring and eliminating unnecessary effort means becoming aware of what you are doing as you go about doing it. The skill to monitor one's own state helps the actor maintain a beneficial consciousness of the self without becoming self-conscious. The actor can learn not to overwork physically, not to misdirect effort or attention, not to let adrenalin or anxiety derail the performance. The actor can learn to create a physicality that contributes to character and does not harm actor. The actor can learn to be open to the moment, to be spontaneous, to be simple. When he no longer creates tension and resistance in order to work, then the actor is simply free to go about the business of the character. Aaron Halva, actor and SMU graduate, realized this during performance one night:

"I had been coping with a deeply rooted pattern of reaction that occurred in my back and shoulders whenever I would speak on stage. This reaction involved unnecessary tension in the lower part of my spine and slight raising of the shoulders. But both actions had psychological counterparts: the gripping in my back gave me a sensation of vocal power and the shoulders rising elicited safety and comfort in front of 'all those people'...It took an incredible amount of will power and a great deal of courage for me to let my voice sail out of my body without overusing my lower back muscles; their overuse was as connected to my character as his shoes....One night I looked over the cliff and fell into the blue: I let myself speak loudly and assuredly to someone on stage without leaving myself and without muscular tension. I felt as naked as the day I was born. I was just a guy walking around fixing watches. I was free."

When he was no longer fighting with himself by creating and then trying to overcome the interfering tension, Halva could simply go about the character's business of fixing watches and answering questions. Actor and character were united in the same moment toward the same objective.

According to Stanslavski, there is a direct connection between the internal need to express and the external expression when the actor does not get in his own way. The Alexander Technique facilitates this essential link in the acting process. The actor's consciousness supports the character's consciousness by taking care of the conditions that free the actor to act and the character to be. This freedom is exciting—when the actor is free anything can happen! The actor is free to embody the character fully. The character is free to intend and to desire and to respond and to choose and to take action. The play comes to life moment by moment, drawing in the audience, the other essential participant in performance, to connect with that truth happening on the stage.

The Alexander Technique in Childbirth

⁊⁊ *by Ilana Machover*

Pregnancy brings with it physical changes that make good use especially important in order to prevent backache and other common symptoms. As the general public's awareness of the Alexander Technique continues to grow, many pregnant women seek the help of Alexander teachers in overcoming some of the discomforts that may accompany pregnancy. What is perhaps less well known—and certainly deserves to be better appreciated—is that the Alexander Technique has a unique contribution to make in the process of childbirth itself.

In F.M. Alexander's day, it was taken for granted in the West that a woman in labor should lie flat on her back. In this unhelpful position, even the Alexander Technique can achieve only very limited results. However, in recent decades it has become widely accepted that a woman in labor should stay upright and move about. Many women nowadays give birth in a supported squat, in the "monkey" position, or on all fours. In this new context it is possible for the Alexander Technique to realize its potential.

Modern medicine has looked for technological fixes, including high-powered drugs, to eliminate pain from childbirth. Paradoxically, by insisting on the supine position in labor, Western medicine actually exacerbated the problem it was ostensibly trying to solve. The drugs developed, especially the epidural anesthesia, are based on the concept of a passive woman lying down throughout her labor. This led to increasing medicalization of birth.

We have to understand the introduction of pain-killing drugs during labor in its historical context: it coincided with great advances in surgery, aided by the invention of antibiotics and other pharmacological remedies. So, when epidural anesthesia began to be used on a mass scale to eliminate labor pains, it was generally regarded as a panacea. It was hoped that women would be able to give birth safely and painlessly.

Indeed, many Western women acquiesce in the medicalization of birth. In matters of health we are conditioned to accept medical authority, to abdicate responsibility and submit to routine procedures. We in the modern Western world generally are not used to pain and have a very low tolerance for it, and this is both a cause and a consequence of the widespread use of painkillers for the slightest discomfort.

But over the years, the negative side-effects of these drugs have become apparent and disappointment has set in. Gradually it was noticed that when painkillers were used, further medical intervention often followed. The rate of births involving forceps and Caesarean section has soared. A British survey, "Health after Childbirth" by the University of Birmingham's Medical School *(HMSO,* 1991) shows links between health problems (subsequent backache, for example) and some delivery procedures, notably epidural anesthesia. There are also effects on the baby. Short-term side-effects are well documented: after all, the baby is born stoned! Are there any long-term side effects? There is not enough research and we do not know much; but what we do know is not good news. A report from Sweden *(Acta obstetricia et gynecologica Scandinavica.* 67, 1988) found that among young drug addicts there was a correlation between the drug they preferred and the drug their mothers had received in childbirth. The authors suggest that this can be explained as an effect of imprinting. Also, the first contact between mother and baby can be disturbed. Some natural reflexes—those of the baby, such as suction, as well as of the mother, such as milk-ejection—can easily be warped, making breast-feeding difficult to establish.

Human birth is a very finely tuned involuntary process that has evolved over many thousands of years. It depends on a series of signals passing between the mother's brain and the rest of her body, and is controlled by the secretion of appropriate hormones for each of its three stages: dilation of the cervix, birth itself, and delivery of the placenta (afterbirth). This physiological process (which has important psychological aspects) can easily be disrupted by any outside interference. But painkillers eliminate pain precisely by masking the body's signals and blocking their pathways; and it is for this reason that they often disrupt the natural course of labor, necessitating further medical intervention.

In recent years, some segments of the natural childbirth movement, alarmed by the negative side-effects of painkilling drugs, have sought ways of lessening the laboring woman's dependence on them. As one of the means to this end they advocate a more active role for the woman—hence the new concept: Active Birth. Since the 1970s, it has become accepted that the force of gravity has an important role to play during the process of birth; so that if the woman stays upright, her labor is facilitated in many ways. Influenced by Alexander's thinking, I understood that in this case, as in all others, it is not just a matter of *what* we do (staying upright), but *how* we do it: using inhibition and direction. In fact, it transpires that our "monkey" is one of the best stances during the whole of labor. "Monkey" is half-way between squatting and standing upright: the feet are wide apart, the knees partly bent, and the upper part of the body tilts over the hip joints; thus the force of gravity aids contractions and makes them stronger and more efficient.

This observation led me to devise a series of movements based on the "monkey" which are useful during contractions. Exploiting the force of gravity is not the only advantage: as a result of the mother leaning forward, her abdominal wall becomes a kind of hammock for the baby, while the tilt of her pelvis makes more space for the baby's head to enter the pelvic brim; thus the baby is encouraged to move into the optimal position for birth. In order to soothe the pain, it is of para-mount importance to move freely, so during labor this position of mechanical advantage ought to be used in a dynamic way: the woman can maintain her primary control while shifting her weight from one leg to the other, either on her own or sup-ported by her partner.

Since many women find it helpful to go on all fours during

labor, I looked for a way of making this stance more dynamic and integrated with the principles of the Alexander Technique. I devised what I call the "pear movement": the woman is on all fours and, with her head leading, her body describes the shape of a pear parallel to the floor. This shape also echoes the outline of the uterus. The pear movement is useful in encouraging her to free her joints and prevent tension from accumulating, especially in the shoulders, arms and lower back. With her neck free and her head leading the movement, her back lengthens and widens, so that it does not sag and create tension in the lumbar area.

"I feel strongly that the Alexander Technique is of great benefit during childbirth and can enable women to have a drug-free, positive experience. . . . I could remain calm and could give directions to my body: making saliva, keeping my neck free, breathing out through a softened mouth, which stopped my body from reacting to the pain by tensing. . . .Your voice was in my head, reminding me of my directions to my body. . . . I spent most of the time doing the 'pear movement' on the gym ball, on all fours, in monkey or lunge with John (transferring our weight from side to side)—ensuring I changed my position often.

"I also feel that the reason I have such a contented, hungry, healthy baby is due to her being born into the world in a natural way without any medical intervention." Stephanie W., March 1995.

Unfortunately, many women who wish to have a natural childbirth do not achieve their wish: at some point during their labor they ask for (or are offered and accept) painkillers. This starts a chain of events which, while being almost inexorable, is unforeseen by the woman herself, leading eventually to further and more drastic medical intervention.

Why do so many women succumb to the temptation of drugs? One of the complaints of the medical profession against the natural childbirth movement is that we encourage women to take a romantic attitude and have unrealistic expectations about their birth experience. I must admit that after reading the literature and attending many classes and seminars run by various childbirth educators, I have come to the conclusion that there is some truth in that complaint. Two inter-related issues are involved here: first, the prevailing attitude to labor pains; secondly, the right tools, skills and means for coping with these pains.

The role of pain in labor has not received enough attention by writers on childbirth. Grantly Dick-Read, a pioneer of the natural childbirth movement, thought that childbirth should not be painful and that only fear and anxiety make it so. Lamaze and other advocates of the psychoprophylactic approach also thought that by teaching women to breathe in a certain way the pain could be eliminated. The medical mainstream as well as most advocates of natural childbirth have so far not recognized that labor pain may in fact be functional and should not be eliminated. Even Michel Odent, one of the most revolutionary leaders of the natural childbirth movement, does not stress the positive function of pain in the mechanism of the *entire* process of birth.

It is now known that during labor, together with the hormone oxytocin (which regulates the contractions) the woman's body releases beta-endorphin, one of its natural opiates. Many childbirth educators stress this fact, implying that it is the natural answer to the problem of labor pains. But in fact it is not the complete answer. Even in the presence of beta-endorphin, labor is painful for most women. That implication also reinforces the mistaken notion that pain in labor is essentially negative and ought to be eliminated by one means or another.

The idea that in order to deal with the pain the woman merely needs to allow her hormones and the primitive part of her brain to take over is part of the romanticization of childbirth, leading many women to have false expectations which are easily frustrated. Then the woman may feel that her body is betraying her.

My special classes for pregnant women are called *Eutokia*, from the classical Greek, meaning happy relaxed childbirth. I tell my students frankly that labor is usually painful, and that the pain is there for a purpose. They should not expect to eliminate it but can learn to cope with it by using the principles of the Technique.

"Even though it was my third baby, I was overwhelmed by the pain. I had forgotten what it was like. I was so glad that in our last meeting you had told us that nothing you could say would describe what the pain was really like. In another prenatal class, they said we should let ourselves open up like a flower. In the event, this proved to be quite unhelpful. Without the willingness to accept the pain, I would not have been able to deal with it." Orna H., March 1995.

"The 'gentle' build-up, from the early morning show to the more difficult contractions, lasted at least ten hours. I used much of this time to practice the movements you taught me, which felt so much like the 'right' movements. I did them to get them clear in my mind: the 'pear', 'monkey' with my hands on the back of a chair, all fours, and some whispered ah's. All of this, plus a Eutokia class the previous day, meant I knew what was available to me when labor became hard. To me, the Eutokia message is to avoid a rut and use all those movements that are helpful. I then felt that I understood the meaning of the Alexander Technique—I was calm, not panicking, I felt relaxed in my body, at home, and did not have to rush. The Alexander Technique is all about these things: being aware of how you move and therefore making those movements less wasteful of energy—vital during labor." Ann G., March 1995.

An influential current in the natural childbirth movement believes that the process of labor is purely instinctual and requires no conscious preparation, merely the creation of conditions in which the animal instincts of the woman are allowed to function undisturbed. In their opinion, under favorable external conditions the laboring woman is able to undo her previous habitual behavior, allowing the primitive part of the brain to assume control. This enables the involuntary process of labor to take its course, regulated by the appropriate hormonal balance.

As a teacher of the Alexander Technique, I realized that things don't quite happen this way. How can we expect our untrained instincts to spring to our rescue during birth? The Technique teaches us to pause and think before acting; Alexander pointed out that evolution has carried humans away from a purely instinctual use of the body, and made us reliant on consciousness. In ordinary everyday activity, we cannot so easily re-establish the primary control and rid ourselves of old habits of misuse: some work of re-education is necessary. This is even more important when pain is present, because pain activates the startle reflex, which tends to heighten tension and exacerbate misuse.

Exactly the same thing applies—and for exactly the same

reasons—to the special activity of childbirth. Emotion, body-use and chemistry are linked and interact with each other. While we cannot control our body chemistry *directly,* we can learn to exercise conscious control over our body use; and this, in turn, can have an effect upon our hormonal balance. A woman in labor receives a clear signal from her body just before the onset of a contraction. This is a cue that ought to be used for inhibition—one of the most important principles of the Technique. But in humans this response to the cue cannot be purely instinctive; it must be learned.

The unique and crucial contribution that the Alexander Technique has to offer to a woman in labor goes far beyond acceptance of pain: it provides her with ways and means for coping with the pain by consciously working with nature rather than against it. A woman can benefit from this unique contribution if she is not only willing to accept pain, but also learns in advance how to take an active role and apply the Technique to the process of childbirth. Without this thinking, all the various exercises and relaxation methods taught in prenatal classes are of limited value, and in some cases are counter-productive, as they may enhance patterns of misuse.

Having learned to move in everyday life without interfering with the primary control, we can apply this skill during contractions. In order to cope with the pain and allow the correct hormonal balance that controls labor to function, we need consciously to inhibit our startle reflex. Instead of flexing, tensing and pulling the head back and down (followed by other symptoms of a panic attack), we can consciously and voluntarily undo the involuntary muscle tension. The residual tension that may remain at the end of a contraction can be dissipated during the interval before the next contraction; this is a good time for "reorganization."

"As soon as I felt one [a contraction] coming on, I would stand and go into a supported 'monkey'. Of all things I did in labor, this seems to have been the best in helping dilation to occur. . . .It was a long labor and I never could have imagined beforehand the pain I experienced. However, by remaining confident that birth is a natural process and with health and the Alexander Technique on my side, I was able to experience childbirth without worry, drugs, intervention—and at home." Penny S., November 1994.

A woman can better deal with the pain by giving herself directions, moving in a relaxed way, and at the same time telling herself again and again that the pain does not indicate that there is something wrong, but that it is functional rather than pathological.

The experience of a drug-free, natural childbirth can be very exhilarating and satisfying for the new mother. To be with one of my students while she is having a baby and applying 'body-learning' the Alexander way is always most rewarding.

"This triumph is not to be won in sleep, in trance, in submission, in paralysis or in anaesthesia, but in a clear, open eyed, reasoning, deliberate consciousness and apprehension of the wonderful potentialities possessed by mankind, the transcendent inheritance of a conscious mind." (Alexander, F.M. *Man's Supreme Inheritance*. Downey: Centerline Press, 1988, p. 41).

Born to Sing

ૐ *by Ron Murdock*

I can't remember a time when I did not sing. My earliest memories are of singing with my mother while she baked bread or did the ironing. I sang my first solo in our church when I was four years old.

I did not begin any formal voice training until my voice broke when I was 14 years old. I grew up in a small village in Nova Scotia and was indeed fortunate to have Vivian Brand, a music educator par excellence, as my first singing teacher. She taught music in the schools in the nearby town. Every child or teenager who came in contact with her could sing because she firmly believed we are born to sing.

When I went to the University, the professor who taught School Music Education impressed upon us that all children, unless something is organically wrong, can sing. She gave us various skills, exercises and ideas, (including "tone matching" games) to use with children who were so-called "droners"— meaning they could not sing in tune. (She also impressed upon us that droners were most often children who had not been sung to at home.) These tone matching games developed and reinforced the coordination between the ear and the larynx—a necessary step because once this is done the child sings in tune. It can be that simple.

I applied these skills when I taught school music in Montreal between the years 1962 and 1966, to children between age 6 and 13. In this four year span, dealing with hundreds of children, there was not one who, eventually, could not sing. At most, it took about three months (one half-hour class lesson per week) of tone matching exercises before all were "in tune" (and usually it took less); in the end they all sang and what fun they had doing so.

Why then are so many people reluctant to sing? Why do they feel they can not sing at all? It is a strange situation, given the fact that children love to sing and their first attempts at speech are singing sounds. And it is even stranger, given that with the right help children can, and want to, sing. In my experience, people who are embarrassed to sing (or who think they cannot sing) almost always were told in school that they had an ugly voice, sang too loudly, that they did not know how to sing or were "droners." They were excluded from class singing or the choir and still feel hurt about it.

Children tend to believe what adults tell them and are, therefore, at the mercy of teachers and parents. If they are told they cannot sing, they will believe it. They will not be able to sing—at least not until their beliefs change. It is cruel to tell a child it does not know how to sing, and people suffer for years because of it. If you are someone this has happened to, then you have been deprived of a right that is as basic and natural as using your hands, skipping, or breathing.

This is a very good example of what F.M. Alexander meant when he said the way we think of a thing influences how we use it. In this case, a child being led to believe he cannot sing influences his ability to sing. On the other hand, the way I was taught to think about children being born to sing enabled me to help them overcome the obstacles that prevented them from singing.

When we come to the training of singers, we see that almost every singing teacher thinks of the voice in a somewhat different way. These various ways of thinking result in just as many "techniques" or "methods" as there are teachers, each one attempting to produce a good sound. These "methods" are then reflected in the physical use of the singer as he attempts to put them into practice. Some approaches to singing are clear and trouble free, resulting in a generally well-coordinated use of the body. Others could not be more difficult, resulting in heavy muscular effort, gasping for breath, and unease.

Despite such varied approaches to singing, it is clear that the end result most singing teachers are looking for is usually the same. A true story illustrates this point: A fine young singer gave a recital at an International Conference of Singing Teachers. At the end of her recital all the singing teachers gave her a standing ovation and most of them said: "Of course she uses my method."! The only way to cut through so many different approaches is to understand what the voice is and how it works.

I think the most important first step to good use of the voice is a desire to communicate. In the introduction to a book called, *Singing: The Physical Nature of the Vocal Organ*, by Professor Frederick Husler and Yvonne Rodd-Marling, Rodd-Marling says, "Singing is a highly physical happening, a unique form of communication produced by muscle-movements set in motion by a fundamentally emotive desire to express beauty."

Everyone communicates their thoughts and feelings each time they speak—day in and day out. Some find it easier than others, but we can safely say we do know how to communicate. Our survival more or less depends on it. However, that singing is a "unique form of communication" should be examined.

What does she mean by unique? The communication level required by anyone who wants to sing well needs to be on a very large scale and to be overtly emotional. It is this exaggerated level of communication of feeling that actually sets in motion and coordinates the vast, complex muscle structures of the singing instrument. This puts a very great physical demand on a professional singer—as great a demand as that of any top athlete.

At this point let us see how Rodd-Marling's definition of singing might change our approach to singing or speaking. Her idea rests on wanting to communicate something and on the desire to express beauty.

Sing a song. Any song you know well. Or take a piece of prose or poetry and read it aloud. Were you aware that as you began to sing or recite, you lost some sense of communication? Perhaps not, but, if you did, then try the following: Have the desire to communicate the mood or feeling of a song/poem to someone else. Keep the desire to communicate the feeling uppermost in your mind. If a friend is working with you, communicate it to her. Otherwise, try looking into your own eyes in a mirror. (Notice that it is your eyes that begin the expression, the feeling. When you smile, the eyes smile first and lead the lips. To begin with, check to see that your eyes are friendly, humorous, warm and welcoming. You can add other emotions later, as you wish.)

Play with this idea for a while and repeat it until you are satisfied you have really communicated some feeling. Now, repeat what you sang, and make sure you want the sound you are making to be as beautiful as possible. Has anything changed? Was it different? Was it easier? Did you begin to get the feeling that somehow "the right thing did itself," as Alexander would say? Did you have a sense that the whole thing was somehow deeper, more complete, more intense? I think you will find that keeping the thought of wanting to communicate and express something beautifully will help make vital changes in your general coordination and will bring about a different and easier use of your body and improve the quality of the sound you are making.

I'm sure Alexander must have had a strong sense of communication and most likely did it automatically. He was, after all, an actor, a performer. Performers want to communicate at this strong level, and do so. It's what motivates them and should motivate anyone working with singers and actors.

It is easy to lose sight of this important aspect of vocal

work when concentrating so heavily on learning new skills, either as a singer practicing vocal exercises or an Alexander teacher absorbed in refining balance and coordination. The temptation to become involved internally with what is going on is very great when so much emphasis is placed on inhibiting old responses and learning any new skill. Therefore it is important that the student maintain a strong connection with the world outside himself. A desire to communicate is a good way to establish this connection.

As Rodd-Marling says in her definition of singing, the vocal and breathing mechanism is set in motion by the desire to express oneself and to communicate. Therefore, including communication in vocal work is absolutely essential to the functioning of the instrument as a whole. Otherwise, singing can become all too difficult and mechanical. It is impossible to control consciously each of the many parts of the whole singing instrument, all of which need to work at the same time in a highly coordinated way. The conscious control wants to be directed at maintaining the poise and direction of the body to allow the voice to emerge by itself.

Without the desire to express something, the vocal organ cannot cooperate and then, if you want to sing, you will have to "do" it. Using the thought that the whole mechanism is set in motion by the desire to communicate helps the singer avoid "doing" and prevents voice work from dwindling into a series of mechanical movements. Why this is so and what that mechanism is in its entirety will become clearer when we have looked at the anatomy.

What, then, is this vast vocal organ? Of what is it made? How does it work? It is an instrument which goes from the crown of the head to the soles of the feet and specifically involves the breathing organ and the larynx. Each of these is made up of many smaller parts, all of which need to be fully awake and active before the "whole" instrument can work together.

Let us take a closer look, starting with the anatomy of the larynx. (Husler's drawings of these parts in his book, *Singing*, are highly recommended.) The larynx is situated at the front of the neck and is made up of three cartilages: 1) a large one which contains the vocal folds, called the shield or thyroid cartilage; 2) a smaller one below, and attached to it, called the ring cartilage; and 3) two pyramid (or arytenoid) cartilages which sit on top of the ring cartilage inside the shield cartilage. The back ends of the vocal cords are attached to the pyramid cartilages. These cartilages are responsible for bringing the vocal cords together.

The shield and ring cartilages are suspended in a sort of "cat's cradle" of muscles. Some muscles connect the larynx to the top of the chest, (anchoring it forward and down), others connect upward to the tongue bone while others attach upward and backward to the soft palate and the head. Yet another muscle connects the back of the larynx to the gullet while another pair run from the shield cartilage to the shoulder. All these muscles form what Husler and Rodd-Marling called an "elastic scaffolding" or suspensory mechanism around the larynx.

At rest, none of this elastic scaffolding is very active and the vocal cords themselves are inactive. During speech, some of the suspensory musculature of the larynx is brought into action and the cords become active. However, only during singing does the whole of this mechanism become fully active. As I learned from Husler and Rodd-Marling, the singing instrument only exists when it is singing. They argued that so little of the instrument is involved during ordinary speech then speech must be an inferior use of the whole instrument. Anatomically it must be, therefore, a singing instrument. Whether the individual chooses or is inclined to use it to sing depends on many factors, one of which I dealt with at the beginning of the chapter.

The fact that people were born with a singing instrument had a profound effect on me when I first heard it 30 years ago and it continues to influence and fascinate me. It is a fact which is usually overlooked when dealing with the voice, but what a powerful tool with which to approach any voice work. First and foremost it means that the singer is always his own instrument. No instrumentalist is faced with such a situation. A cello is always a cello. The instrument is always there. The same applies to all the other instruments. Yes, the instrumentalist should learn how to maintain his own body poise and direction in relationship to the instrument. He is an extension of the instrument, but the instrument itself is not wholly dependent on him—mind, body and soul—for its shape and form. The voice, however, is the exception. A singer has to establish the "poise and direction" and the shape of his instrument each time he sings and it is entirely susceptible to his moods and thoughts.

The entire suspensory mechanism exerts a stabilizing force on the shield, ring and arytenoid cartilages which, in turn, stabilize the vocal cords as they lie, stretched front to back, inside the shield cartilage. This intricate relationship of muscles is affected positively when the head is allowed to be free on the neck. Each muscle achieves its proper length and connection with the other in an optimum state for functioning well. The muscles work together, each set meeting the opposing pull of the other which allows the larynx to become poised, balanced and properly suspended. The vocal cords are actively lengthened and stretched by this action and thus brought closer together. In these favorable conditions they can close properly to execute the sound quickly and efficiently and thereby produce a clear, clean tone with a minimum of effort. The throat is properly open—in Alexander terms, "lengthened and widened."

If the cords do not close properly, then the tone sounds breathy, husky, limited, uncomfortable and powerless to both performer and listener. There is then a great temptation to make extra effort to achieve more power by increasing the air pressure. If this state is not corrected the cords will soon begin to produce a protective mucous covering which makes for a very uncomfortable feeling in the throat and sounds unpleasant. Singers call such mucous a "frog in the throat."

The application of extra air pressure is often accompanied by greater physical effort involving poor coordination between the muscles of the ribs, back, arms, and legs, and a considerable collapse in the torso. This is poor "use" of the body indeed. If the use of excess air pressure is allowed to continue it can lead to the formation of polyps or nodules on the inside edges of the cords. This can feel like a sore throat, a permanent feeling of "frogs in the throat," hoarseness, or all three. The tone will be husky, unclear and weak. In some cases these growths have to be removed surgically.

Another result of a poorly erected and suspended vocal organ is that it can give rise to top notes cracking or the voice breaking. Because of undue tension in the neck, one (or more) of the suspensory muscles will not be in balance with the others and, robbed of its proper length, does not have enough strength to keep directed when singing a top note. The healthy tension in the vocal cords needed for top notes (which is dependent on the stability of the elastic scaffolding) is thereby suddenly and dramatically reduced and the note sounds as if it has cracked or split. The muscle gives way much the same as when a tent peg suddenly pulls part-way out of the ground. The tension in the guy ropes lets go and the tent sags. However drastic a cracking note may sound it by no means signals the end of a career. It simply means more training is necessary.

There are several other areas of direct interference with the larynx which are potentially hazardous to the suspensory mechanism. For instance, if the lower jaw is pulled back and/or stiff, then the tongue and the laryngeal suspensory muscles attached to the tongue bone will also be stiff. This resulting stiffness is passed on from the jaw through the tongue to the larynx and thus to the vocal cords, and renders them less powerful.

Another form of interference to the suspensory muscles is caused by the mistaken idea many singers have that an open throat (which all agree is necessary for singing) involves lifting the soft palate upward while pushing downward with the back of the tongue. A quick look at the anatomy will tell us what happens if the tongue is pushed downward. The shield cartilage is attached to the underside of the tongue bone (hyoid) while the tongue is attached to the top side. If the tongue is then pulled backward and down onto the hyoid bone the entire structure is forced downward onto the top of the shield cartilage and this destroys the balancing upward pull of the attached suspensory muscles. All the other suspensory muscles are thrown out of balance, the back of the throat is completely blocked by the tongue and the vocal cords are quite literally crushed by the action. Their function is greatly impaired and the result is a loss of tone quality, range and power. The sound is throaty and lacking in resonance. This is one of the most common problems found in singing and is referred to as depression of the larynx.

A throat in such a condition (where the larynx is not properly suspended, the whole structure is cramped by a head pulled back on a stiff neck and the larynx depressed) would look, on the inside, like a collapsed suspension bridge with cables (the elastic scaffolding) twisted in every direction and the actual roadway of the bridge (the vocal cords) rendered useless. It is as difficult to try to sing with a buckled suspensory vocal mechanism as it would be to drive over that collapsed bridge.

A throat is truly open when all the suspensory muscles are working freely in balance, the vocal cords are lengthened and approximating well, the tongue and palate muscles are released and all this is fully coordinated with the organ of breathing. In fact, the organ of breathing contributes greatly to the ability of the laryngeal muscles to release properly. In this condition the soft palate is indeed raised, but not at the expense of the surrounding tissues and muscles. The sound is improved by the action because it occurs in balance with the other parts. We could therefore say that a throat is fully open when we allow the head to be free on the neck—providing there are no other subtle interferences from the surrounding muscles.

Because of the connection between the jaw, tongue and laryngeal muscles with the soft palate, freedom in the lower jaw results in freedom of the soft palate. The arch can widen and lift properly because it is not being dragged down by any stiffness in the muscles attached to it. (The lower jaw and tongue are released by Alexander's whispered "Ah," and the palatial arch widened by the direction, "Think of something funny to make you smile." This is one reason why the whispered "Ah" is such an excellent corrective and restorative vocal exercise.) The head resonators are opened by these releases and the sound is free to be amplified there. This lift and width exerts an important pull upward and backwards on the larynx which is perfectly balanced by the forward and downward pull of the two large muscles attaching the larynx to the chest.

What effect does poise and direction of the head balancing on the top of the spine (and therefore poise and direction in the larynx) have on the tone? First and foremost it helps focus the tone because it aids the lengthening and approximation of the vocal folds. This helps the voice project, sound forward and high, round, full, and more colorful, all of which are qualities held as "ideal" in the singing world.

All the musculature discussed so far plays an important role in "support." That is to say, there is much more to the idea of "support" for the voice than just the commonly held idea of "diaphragm support" or "breath support" or, heaven forbid, "stomach support." In fact, I like to think of the word "support" (in this context) as a word that describes the action that takes place when all the muscles are in balance and working together in harmony. Paradoxically the more you try to support directly, the less results you get.

In Alexander terms, freeing the head and neck prevents the collapse of the vocal suspensory mechanism and ensures a healthy environment in which the tone can be produced. Thus the suspensory and vocal muscles are allowed to reach their proper length, ready to work with maximum efficiency. This is the state the vocal mechanism *is* in, in fact wants to be in, when it is not interfered with. It is indeed a wonderful effect when nature is enforced in this way. When the singing mechanism is poised and balanced, free and ready to function properly, the student is then well prepared for a good singing teacher who can hear how and where the instrument needs training in order to balance the many parts to work as a whole. The instrument can only function properly when the whole structure is in balance, especially the critical head-neck relationship.

The breathing organ makes up the other half of the singing instrument. Like the vocal organ, the breathing organ has a suspensory mechanism which needs attention to ensure its poise, balance and direction. It too has to be erected, ready to work, because in most people it is usually collapsed. And in comparison to the vocal mechanism, the musculature of the breathing organ is larger and more powerful—capable of doing a lot of good if in proper condition, and equally capable of doing a lot of mischief if not.

Perhaps one of the most important muscle groups to be aware of in the breathing organ is sacrospinalis. These muscles extend from the back of the skull all the way down to the base of the spine in a series of connecting muscles. It is these long series of muscles in the back which, when encouraged to lengthen by freeing the head, are most responsible for the erection and stability of the breathing organ. When these muscles are encouraged to reach their proper length, the entire torso is suspended, the student lengthens in stature, the intercostal arch opens and widens allowing the diaphragm to move freely without unnecessary effort which permits the breath to enter the lungs easily.

As the head goes forward and up, the tail bone (and with it

the pelvis) needs to release in the opposite direction in order for sacrospinalis to lengthen. This movement is only possible when the hip joints, knee and ankle joints are free. The weight of the head and pelvis pulling in opposite directions is what encourages the sacrospinalis muscle groups to lengthen. (Pulling, in this case, is a physiological action based on a thought, not a direct pull like you might do in trying to open a stuck door). The answering and opposite movement of the pelvis to the head direction is necessary, otherwise it is like trying to stretch an elastic band without holding both ends.

As the pelvis releases, the lower abdominal muscles come into play and are strengthened by being taken inward and slightly upward toward the back by the movement of the pelvis. The tonus of these muscles is extremely important because they are responsible for maintaining the position and release of the diaphragm. This movement in turn frees up the rib cage and allows the full flexibility of movement of it. In that condition the diaphragm is truly released and free. If an Alexander Teacher did nothing else for a singer than help her achieve lengthening of the back muscles, he will have achieved a great deal.

It is an unfortunate fact that many common ideas about breathing have a devastating impact on the organ of breathing, rather than achieving increased freedom of it. Many people are taught to breathe in by pushing the lower abdomen (especially the area between the belly button and pubic bone) down and out with a combination of breath pressure and distention of the dome of the diaphragm. It is done in a mistaken attempt to "breathe low" and to "support," and seems to have evolved as an answer to breathing too high up in the chest and raising the shoulders to do so.

Such low breathing results in an over-use, collapse, and distention of the lower abdominal muscles, and results in a severe collapse of the torso and the diaphragm, a pulling in of the lower back, stiffening in the pelvic muscles and legs, and a heavy shortening of the muscles at the front of the body. This makes any lateral movement of the ribs impossible, and such misuse has exactly the opposite effect of what is desired. The situation becomes more complicated because once the lower abdominal muscles are pushed outward on the in-breath, they then have to be pulled inward as the singer begins to sing. The whole process becomes full of effort and involves more and more "doing." The semi-reflex action of the in-breath cannot work and then the singer has to make considerable effort to get the next breath. It is a time-consuming and totally inefficient way of using the breathing organ.

If we would just stop a minute and think, it is clear there is no way breath can enter the area behind the lower abdominal muscles. The intestines, the bladder and, in the female, the uterus and ovaries lie here. The breath goes into the lungs which are inside the rib cage—a long way from the lower abdomen. Of course, there is *movement* in the lower abdomen, as a result of the air coming into the lungs and the downward movement of the diaphragm, which slightly displaces the organs in the abdomen. Left on its own this causes no difficulties with the general poise of the mechanism. However, when this action is exaggerated and deliberately interfered with, complications set in causing loss of poise and direction.

Of course, there has to be a *release* of the lower abdominal muscles and a connection right through to the basin of the pelvis; otherwise, the diaphragm cannot fully release. However, this release and connection can happen in a much more efficient way, with far more effective results, than crudely pushing downward and outward with breath pressure and the diaphragm.

Each one of these problems is caused by a misconception that negatively influences how the system is then used. What we want is the two opposing movements of the head going forward and up and the tail going forward and down (which helps anchor the stem of the diaphragm, attached as it is on the inside of the lumber spine) and to encourage the back to lengthen and widen so the rib-cage is free and the floating ribs can move.

Alexander called this "direction," and when it happens the connection and opening to the lower abdomen is immediately available with little effort and maximum effect.

With these directions active, one can then look at the other five main sets of breathing-out muscles: the latissimus dorsi (two large muscles in the back), the rectus abdominus, which runs from the pubic bone to the chest, the inner and outer obliques, the upper-inner chest muscle (a butterfly-shaped muscle under the chest), and the intercostals (in between the ribs). *All* these muscles play an important role in helping the singer breathe out. The extent of the breathing organ goes far beyond the one set of lower abdominal muscles which so often are the only ones to receive any attention. Unless all the muscles involved are working together then any one set will have to work very hard indeed, and the entire organism is thrown out of balance. When all the muscles do work together, singing becomes a fluent, easy, exhilarating event for both performer and listener.

If you want to breathe *in* properly you need to attend to breathing *out* fully. If you want to breathe out fully, then you need to have at your disposal such a use of the entire breathing mechanism as I have just described. It is vital to remember that none of this requires "doing" but it does clearly involve intent. You cannot expect to stand there with nothing happening and hope that somehow it will all work. You need to be clear what it is you want, really desire it to happen, and then make sure nothing interferes with it.

Working rhythmically is an excellent way to activate the mechanism without "doing," as the muscles respond easily to such movement. If the out-breath is accomplished fully and rhythmically, using all the muscle groups outlined here, and there is no stiffening of the neck, shortening in stature, or pulling down in front, then the in-breath can happen as a reflex action to fill the vacuum created by the out-breath. This is how it is designed to work in the first place. You are then working fully with nature and what is more, you are strengthening it. Treated this way the breathing organ responds favorably, cooperates, and gives the singer the impression he has to do less and less to get more and more. The in-breath then encourages and stimulates even more lengthening in the torso and the whole thing becomes self-generating.

When this happens, and only when this happens, the movements in the organ of breathing and the vocal organ coordinate and it can then (and only then) be said that the tone, the voice, is "supported." Stiffen the neck, legs, or rib cage, and the coordination is interrupted, resulting in diminished support. Support results from all the necessary muscle actions working together rather than from a direct action of any one set of muscles.

I have deliberately left any detailed discussion of the diaphragm until late in this chapter for a number of reasons. I wanted to establish very clearly that if the structure in which the diaphragm is housed is properly maintained, then the diaphragm will do what it should do by itself in response to the emotional and physical demand placed on it. There is absolutely no need for "diaphragm strengthening exercises"—indeed, there is no need for so-called "diaphragmatic breathing"—both terms which ensure, in their very terminology, "doing" in the Alexander sense. By "doing" I mean any direct interference that destroys much of the playful, delicate, strong action of the diaphragm when it is free.

The breathing-in action of the diaphragm is so strong, so insistent, it will pull the body out of shape unless the scaffolding around it is well activated and maintained. That the diaphragm plays a most important part in the act of singing is without question and, from the point of view of good use of the body, it is far better to learn to leave the poor thing alone and concentrate on the "means whereby" we can get the most effect from it.

The diaphragm is a very large, dome-shaped muscle that fills the rib-cage front to back and from side to side. The stem of it is anchored on the inside of the lumbar spine where it rises to the uppermost dome quite high in the chest (at about the fourth rib or about nipple level in a male). The bottom edges of the lungs and the heart rest on top of it. It flips over to attach on the inside front edge of the ribs just above the point where the ribs separate, and the bottom edges attach to the lower ribs. There is connective tissue from the top of the diaphragm to the back and neck muscles, which helps suspend it from above. Just as the diaphragm can be sucked down out of position and distended by the lower abdominal organs in a state of collapse, so the diaphragm can push these organs out of position and cause a collapse from above if these connective tissue attachments are not erected. Freeing the head on the neck to allow the back to lengthen and widen establishes this erection in the same way as it allows the erection of the elastic scaffolding surrounding the larynx. Therefore, an avoidance of both states of collapse of the diaphragm is what an Alexander teacher helps bring about in the singer by helping him lengthen and widen the back.

When these connective tissues are collapsed, the lower abdominal muscles become distended and over-react to correct the imbalance. The singer knows, instinctively, that some part of his instrument is not in balance and he makes extra effort, by "doing," to compensate. I think the wording found in some passports is very apt when considering the diaphragm. We should "allow the bearer," (in this case, the diaphragm) "to pass freely without let or hindrance, and to afford the bearer such assistance and protection as may be necessary."

The diaphragm is much more than a mechanical shifter of air. It is, above all, a muscle of emotional expression. Everyone has had experiences of just how infectious it can be when someone nearby suddenly and spontaneously laughs. We usually laugh right along with them. Why? Because there is a physiological response in the diaphragm that causes it to react in sympathy with what is being expressed by someone else. This brings us back to Rodd-Marling's definition of singing, and the importance of wanting to express emotion. If the diaphragm is thought of only as a pump then such thinking will greatly diminish the function of it and limit its invaluable contribution to singing. The singer, indeed, then will have to develop a breathing technique to compensate for the lack of spontaneous and reflex action in the diaphragm.

When singing, it is important that the tonus of the diaphragm muscle be high—in other words, we want this strong and vital muscle as our ally. Anatomist V.E. Negus, in his book, *The Comparative Anatomy and Physiology of the Larynx*, states, "If the volume of air (in the lungs) is low then the diaphragm's tonus is high." Conversely, if the volume of air in the lungs is high then the tonus of the diaphragm will be low. In other words, there is a good reason a singer should not take in great amounts of air. Not only is so much air unnecessary, it weakens the diaphragm and thus interrupts the coordination between the diaphragm and voice. As well, too much breath weakens the ability of the vocal cords to close, resulting in a very poor tone. The method of breathing I mentioned earlier (where the lower abdominal wall is pushed down and out on the in-breath) almost guarantees that there will be too much air in the lungs and therefore too little tonus in the diaphragm.

Left to its own devices, the larynx draws the amount of air it needs from the lungs and regulates the emission of it. The amount of air needed is quite small. I think it was the great German soprano Elisabeth Schumann who said she took no more breath to sing than she took to smell a rose. The English soprano Maggie Teyte, who had quite a small but beautiful voice, always said, "Never sing louder than lovely," advice that guarantees the singer will not over-breathe. Trying to take a deep breath is the quickest way to destroy the integration, balance and poise of the entire mechanism.

Whenever possible, when time permits during singing, the singer should be encouraged to allow the air to enter through the nose. For one thing, it prevents too much air being taken in. From a health point of view, the air is warmed and cleaned as it enters the nose and thus affords a natural protection to the lungs. In addition, breathing through the nose is the most efficient way of releasing the contraction in the muscles surrounding the ribs when breathing out. If the next breath is to enter as quickly and easily as a singer needs it to, this tension must be released at the end of the out breath, and released quickly.

When thinking of allowing the breath to enter the nose, imagine the nostril openings are at the inside edges of the eyes on either side of the nose. Starting at this high point, allow the points to widen and imagine that the air enters at this level. The air enters very calmly and easily because the nostrils are widened and not restricted by any collapse. You will not be tempted to over-breathe and take in too much air, the muscles around the ribs release quickly, the breath may feel slightly cool and refreshing, and it will be easier to maintain your direction and poise which, as we well know, establishes the shape of the breathing organ.

It is important to remember that it is the release of the muscles around the rib cage (which allow the diaphragm to release and descend) that draws in the air. Be very sure not to look for release of the muscles around the rib cage by pushing outwards on them with a large intake of air.

In spite of these benefits of breathing in through the nose there are going to be times when it is almost impossible to do so—when singing certain phrases in some of Bach's arias, for example. So many of them are written as if the voice was a string instrument that is not dependent on air. (Even so, string players also need to learn to breathe out while playing). In such cases, there is no other way to let the air in except through the mouth. Providing there is no loss of physical direction, and the singer has trained the breathing organ well so there is no gasping or sucking in of the breath, the occasional breath through the mouth should not cause much difficulty. Gasping for breath is almost always the result of loss of direction in the body. There are even times when it is effective to allow the listener to hear an intake of breath during singing. This is when the singer wishes the audience to feel the emotion of what is coming in the next phrase. When done well, it is not gasping or destructive but very, very communicative.

To sum up, the whole breathing organ joins with the whole vocal organ to form the singing instrument and produce sound. The many parts of both need to be awakened and developed, and maintained in an optimum condition in order to function efficiently, well, and for many years. The only way these two vast mechanisms can hope to coordinate properly is via a strong desire to communicate emotion and express beauty. There is no doubt whatsoever that the entire process is greatly aided, and kept in good working order, by freeing the head and neck while allowing the back to lengthen and widen.

If you proceed with the clear understanding of how the voice works—that it is designed to "sing," and that it is all set in motion by the desire to communicate and express beauty—and you combine this understanding with a balanced "use of the self," a lot of the problems you meet will sort themselves out. In the process, you will understand more and more that we are, indeed, born to sing.

Grabbing the Bird by the Tale

ॐ *by Alex Murray*

Thé native and unspoiled attitude of childhood, marked by ardent curiosity, fertile imagination, and love of experimental inquiry, is near, very near to the attitude of the scientific mind." John Dewey, Preface to *How We Think*, 1910.

ॐ ॐ ॐ ॐ ॐ

"The spontaneity of childhood is a delightful and precious thing, but in its original naive form it is bound to disappear. Emotions become sophisticated unless they become enlightened, and the manifestation of sophisticated emotion is in no sense genuine self-expression. True spontaneity is henceforth not a birth-right but the last term, the consummated conquest of an art, the art of conscious control, to the mastery of which Mr. Alexander's book so convincingly invites us." John Dewey, Preface to *Man's Supreme Inheritance*, 1918.

෨ ෨ ෨ ෨ ෨

My own life-long interest in music was sown in me by my mother, who could play on the piano any melody she heard, and by my father, who introduced me to the penny whistle as soon as I could hold one. Musical curiosity pushed me in my mother's direction and I discovered very early how to play tunes "by ear" on the piano as well as on the penny-whistle.

In the window of the local music shop was a wooden recorder which I coveted but could never afford (it would have cost six months' pocket money). It seemed to me, at age ten, the most superior form of penny whistle. Not many months later, in June of 1940, opportunity knocked. By this time, however, the recorder had taken second place in my affections to a wooden fife.

Believing invasion to be imminent, the British Government initiated a scheme to evacuate children to the Dominions. Enrollment lasted for a brief three weeks, during which time my parents arranged for me to live with my aunt in South Africa. Prior to my departure, I did the rounds of my home-town relations collecting pocket money for the journey. I concealed enough of this from my parents to purchase the much-coveted fife. I remember sitting on my bed, trying to elicit a tune from it and pretending it was just one of my penny whistles.

On the ship to South Africa, with 300 other children, we would gather every evening for a sing-song which I would accompany on the fife or whistle when appropriate. By the time we arrived in Cape Town I was able to play both with equal facility. As we had cases of measles on board, we were kept in quarantine at the Governor General's House, Westbrook. During this period, the Municipal Cape Town Orchestra played for us. During the intermission I spoke to the youngest member of the flute section, a 21 year-old Englishman, David Sandeman. "I play the flute too," was my opening line. He asked me to show him my instrument—very different from his—and invited me to visit him when I settled with my aunt and uncle.

After my first visit and lesson, I was in possession of a real flute, on which he had started his career. I was invited weekly for a free lesson which always concluded with tea and donuts in the company of his mother, a teacher of French in a girls' school, who had recently arrived from England.

Many years later, David Sandeman, who had returned after

the war to become principal flute in the London Philharmonic, gave my wife an account of my lessons with him. He related that I was his first pupil ever and that he was under the impression that there was nothing to teaching the flute—You told the student what needed to be done and he would come back the following week doing it. It wasn't until he had his second student that he discovered there was more to it.

David's approach to teaching the flute was perfectly suited to me. He encouraged me to teach myself—to learn how to learn. He practiced William James's cardinal rule: Never discourage; discouragement is of the devil. This fruitful relationship lasted a year, by which time my uncle was transferred to Johannesburg and I was musically on my own.

As luck would have it, David's orchestra came to Johannesburg for an opera season and I renewed our friendship. During his stay, he introduced me to the Professor of Music at Wits University. He invited me, age 13, to play in the University Orchestra.

On one occasion, we played for the visiting Cape Town Ballet, whose repertoire included the *Carnival of the Animals* by Saint-Saëns. This remains indelibly in my memory because of the virtuosic flute solo, the Aviary. In little over a minute, the player is required to synchronize breath, fingers and tongue, the latter articulating rapidly the syllables teketeketekete over 300 times—a technique known to wind-players as "double-tonguing." At 14, I had not yet attempted to teach myself this skill, having been told by David Sandeman that it was first necessary to master "single-tonguing" (the rapid reiteration of tetetete). In the performance, I think I played the notes minus the articulation—less of a flutter than the composer intended.

During my studies at the Paris Conservatoire from 1950-52, I was once again confronted by the "Aviary," which I took in my stride, double-tonguing and all. Several years later, with the London Symphony, I was called upon to record it as backing to the Ogden Nash verses, recited by Bee Lillie. This version, instead of lasting one minute, was doubled in length, which entailed over 600 repetitions of teke. As an aside, Saint-Saëns's *Volière* is only one of many pieces in which the flute represents our feathered friends. I sometimes ask, in Doctoral exams, that the student write on the ornithological aspects of the flute. A cursory search of my memory recalls the following recordings I made with the London Symphony Orchestra between 1955 and 1967: *Lo Here the Gentle Lark*, the *Gypsy and the Bird* (Joan Sutherland); *Bluebird* in *Sleeping Beauty* (Pierre Monteux); *Pastoral Symphony* (Josef Krips); *Respighi—The Birds* (Dorati); *Firebird* (Stravinsky); *Le Rossignol* (Dorati); the Morceau de Concours for my 1st prize at the Paris Conservatoire in 1952 was Messaien's *Merle Noir* (Blackbird).

Over fifty years after my first acquaintance with the piece, I found myself again confronted with fluttering like a bird while playing in the Sinfonia da Camera (Hobson) in Urbana, Illinois. As with athletic skills, rapid movements are seemingly more suited to the young in years than the long in the tooth. Faced with rapid repeated tongue movements I began to wonder whether my tongue had loosened over the years or whether its mechanism was deteriorating.

Try the following experiment. Divide a regular pulse of one second into three parts (as in a waltz). Count 1-2 of the 1-2-3 and maintain a pulse of 1-(2) 1-(2) 1-(2) beating time on the one only. This will give you a pulse of 90 to the minute. At this speed repeat the syllables tetetete—four tes to a beat. Then intersperse ke between each te (maintaining the four tes to a beat). Thus: you come up with teketeketeketeke and you will have the articulation problem to which I have been referring. This is the "tongue-twister" set by Camille Saint Saëns.

As you will have inferred, except for my very positive experiences with my first teacher, David Sandeman, I consider myself largely self-taught. I did make one disastrous effort to learn the flute from a teacher whose approach was: If you want to study with me, you must do as I say. From his vantage point, everything I had done previously was wrong. To breathe, I must raise my chest like a pouter pigeon. My lips should be fixed in a permanent smile and my tongue must strike the palate audibly to begin each note. Raising the chest to breathe in was one of the erroneous preconceived ideas with which Alexander had to contend in the early days of his teaching. Fixing the lips in a permanent smile is perhaps worse in that it is tantamount to fixing the head at the atlanto-occipital joint. Adding the uncustomary (and unnecessary) movement of the tongue was an overload for my nervous system. Assiduous practice on these lines precipitated a nervous breakdown, one of the symptoms of which was a stutter every time I pronounced the syllable te.

I am still recovering from that teacher's influence. The loss of a natural skill led, in my case, to a tendency unduly to analyze and criticize myself and others. Trying to be right when you have lost the belief in your own rightness (an important ingredient in the make-up of a performing artist) is a double bind. In contrast to the way this teacher taught, a very good friend told me *his* teaching was based on the question: "What is preventing this person from playing well?"

Foreign service in the Royal Air Force put an end to my studies with this teacher and I returned to finding my own way.

Early in my professional civilian career, in 1954, I was introduced to the Alexander Technique and lost no time in trying to apply the principles (as I understood them) to playing the flute. When I began lessons, I was principal flute of the Royal Opera, a strenuous occupation, entailing long rehearsals (10am-3pm) on occasion, with performances every evening and an afternoon performance on Saturday. During the rehearsals in the orchestra pit, there was frequently a cold breeze blowing through the theatre while the scenery was being transported from the street to the stage. I had a tendency to bronchitis which was aggravated by such working conditions. A friend suggested that Charles Neil, one of the members of Alexander's first training course, might be able to help with my respiratory problems. I began a three year course of lessons. I regret to say that what I learned at that time is not what I now understand to be the Alexander Technique. When Charles Neil died in 1958, my Alexander lessons began, and with them, the process of change in my conception of the Technique, my use and, of course, my breathing.

My earliest recollections of applying what I was learning to playing was (and continues to be) to rid the mind of "taking a breath" to play. This is an important aspect of all my practicing. If I wish to play a long phrase, I first exhale, then allow the breath to return (through the nostrils, silently) and then play when the breath is ready to move out. When playing continuously, I always take time to breathe, even if it means stopping the flow of the music. Naturally, this applies to practice. When one is performing, one does what the music requires with whatever means one has at the time.

This kind of practice paid its first real dividends in the late

1950's, when I was the principal flute for the London Symphony. We played an annual Beethoven Cycle with Josef Krips. I found that I was able to play a loud, continuous section of the first Allegro in the 7th Symphony without being aware of "taking a breath." The breath was returning in the brief intervals between the rhythmic figures. Some idea of what happens when you stop the interference can be experienced if you exhale quickly, blowing out the cheeks. Repeat this little experiment rhythmically several times and you will notice that the breath returns with a sort of "elastic recoil."

The next really significant change in my playing was triggered by Alexander's 1906 article, in which he names the great principle in practical respiratory re-education to be *antagonistic action*. The other clue in this article was, "Many people can acquire fair chest poise at the end of inspiration, but... at the end of the expiration the mechanism is absolutely disorganized." I was practicing some difficult passages on my flute at the time, using two mirrors for visual feedback. In my customary way, I divided the long opening phrase into sub-phrases, played them with time for breaths and then, finally, decided to "deflate" and "inflate" myself several times prior to playing the whole phrase in one breath. As I got to the end of the phrase, I saw myself visibly shorten—the pelvis moving forward over the feet, the back "narrowing in the loins." This was the first time in my practice that I had really made an unusual demand on my respiratory capacity and I saw in what way my mechanism was "absolutely disorganized." I then played the same passage but inhibited the movement forward of the pelvis, maintaining my length, and found that I had just as much air as before, but that at the end of the expiration the inspiration took place by "elastic recoil." This to me exemplified *antagonistic action.*

The next really significant evolution in my playing developed out of questions related to the balance of the head, raised by Professor and Alexander teacher Frank Pierce Jones' Psychological Revue article of 1965. This article led me to the writings of Anatomist Raymond Dart—initially "The Postural Aspect of Malocclusion." Jones stated that the center of gravity of the head corresponds roughly to the "sella turcica," an area at the anterior of the base of the skull. I reasoned that the center of gravity must be dependent on the relationship of the upper and lower jaw—which was a mobile one. Free movement of the jaw is integral to the kind of flute playing in which I was interested.

The discoveries I have made over the years have dramatically altered my flute playing. They have also affected my teaching, despite the fact that I do not teach my flute students the Alexander Technique. If they are interested, they can study that on their own initiative (with my encouragement). My personal approach to teaching is to accept the student as he/she is, see what I think can be improved and look for a step-wise progression in the right direction. No matter how badly one plays, one can always play worse; this establishes the negative direction on a continuum. To move from worse to better is the immediate goal. How far is in the lap of the gods. In practicing, I always ask that the student take time to breathe inaudibly, no matter how long, and divide the music into phrases which can be played without strain in one breath. Problems of fingering are broken down into the smallest division—moving from one note to the next. Step 1: Finger note x, think of the fingering for note y. Step 2: Count 1-2-3 and move on 3 from x to y as quickly as possible. Repeat sequence as required. Step 3: Finger and play x; Step 4: Count 1-2-3 and move to y (as short as possible). Step 5: Integrate notes prior to x, pause on x, count and play y. Step 6: Cut duration of pause (progressively). If you think you are about to make a mistake, STOP. Every mistake practiced is a mistake learned. AMEN.

A book appeared some 20 years ago written by a former concert pianist turned computer scientist (*Sentics: The Touch of the Emotions* by Dr. Manfred Clynes). He had investigated the different time-space patterns made by someone pressing their finger on a sensitive button in response to a stimulus designed to elicit an emotional response. The button was able to register time and direction. For example, Hate had a sharp profile and took little time to express, Love by contrast, had a gentler profile and required more time. He named the characteristic form of each emotion its essentic form. He also experimented with the expressive patterns of musical phrases. One of his most useful observations which reinforced something I already thought but had not formulated was that only one emotion can be conveyed at a time. Aggressive movements while playing affectionate music will not result in the sum of the parts but in the expression of one or other (inadequately).

A recent study of the early years of Alexander's development (Rosslyn McLeod, *Up from Down Under*) led me to Francois Delsarte (1811-1872), whose system was taught and advertised by Alexander in 1900 as "an aesthetic science with the same precision as mathematical science." Delsarte's history parallels both Alexander's and my own. A talented youth with a beautiful tenor voice, he was admitted to the Paris Conservatoire at age 14. After six months of vocal instruction his voice was ruined. He remained for four years, studying dramatic art, during which time he realized that his various teachers were each working according to their own personal tastes without any common principle. He set about searching for a scientific basis to artistic expression and from his observations developed his own system of dramatic expression, which he taught for many years in a course of "Applied Aesthetics." In this, he emphasized the true nature of all art, "body," "mind" and "soul."

Since losing my metaphorical voice, my flute playing has taken many turns, but I rediscovered the joy of "playing" when I crossed paths with Chung-Liang Huang, a Tai Chi master and author of *Embrace Tiger and Return to Mountain*. We met as fathers of daughters at a mid-western grade-school when we were talked into performing together for the children (our own included). I discovered that dancing and playing simultaneously, undertaken in the spirit of "play," was both possible and pleasurable. Now, when I sit motionless in an orchestra, it is because I choose to. I know the potential for moving naturally is still there but restrained by choice, not by anxiety.

In my most recent attempts at playing the Aviary, I discovered that, in keeping with a flexible relationship of the jaw, lips and tongue (as examined in the familiar whispered ah), the second syllable of the double-tongue (ke) can be produced in a variety of ways. If you listen carefully to the pitch of a whispered ah and compare it to a whispered eh and then ee, you will notice a rise in pitch as the tongue approaches the palate. The various flutters in the Aviary are in the three different registers of the flute's range. Applying this discovery to the use of the tongue in the different registers, I am able to play the solo more distinctly and more easily than hitherto.

As a final experiment, repeat the following at a speed of 90 beats per minute: tikitikitikitiki/tikitikitikitiki/teketeketeketeke /teketeketeketeke/ takatakatakataka/ takataketi. Repeat four times, non-stop.

My own painful experience led me indirectly to the Alexander Technique and to the constant rebirth of curiosity. I hope yours will encourage you to experiment with the articulation problems of Saint-Saëns's *Aviary*, which are only one aspect of playing such music in an aesthetically satisfying way.

Curiosity may have killed the cat, but it has liberated Saint-Saëns's cage of birds for yet another free flight.

Grief

❧ *by Vivien Schapera*

G rief is an intense and impure emotion. It is colored by sadness, fear, anger, shock, bitterness, frustration, loneliness and pain, but it is bigger still than all of these. We experience grief when we lose something precious, when we lose a loved one. Because we love, we all experience grief at some time in our lives. Some of us suffer many losses and consequently endure much grief.

A few years ago, I was walking in a shopping mall when I glimpsed a sad figure. The stiff back, bowed head and wooden walk broadcast to me, an experienced "reader of bodies," a fresh grief experience. My first response was compassion, my second, surprise. The image was my own reflection in a mall mirror. I was so physically altered by the news that my uncle had died that I had not even recognized myself.

I am no stranger to grief. I have experienced it myself and I have worked with grief in many different forms: people who are terminally ill and their family members; parents who have lost children; and young adults who lost a parent when they were still children.

Mortality is not the only cause of grief. The death of trust, dreams and hopes also leads to traumatic grief experiences. I have seen women who have been sexually abused as children lead a life of prolonged mourning and yearning for the age of innocence; people injured in car accidents who mourn their health and vigor; and lonely people who mourn a former marriage or relationship.

One thing is common to all—grief is a live, raw pain in the heart that weighs us down. We struggle to survive our loss and in that process we clench and tighten. Grief leaves its unmistakable tracks.

Often the emotion is focused into one particularly stressful symptom which cannot be ignored. I am reminded of the artist who came to me with an incapacitating frozen shoulder. She was a gentle, soft-spoken person who outwardly seemed content, her life in good order, everything in its place. As she freed herself from the layers of tension which bound her body, she surprisingly also decided to leave her marriage and to start a new life. I found out later that as a young bride her husband had compelled her to make a traumatic decision with irrevocable consequences.

Another student demonstrated extraordinary neck tension, a grip so fierce that my hands seemed repelled. When her muscles released, it quickly became apparent that she had a great investment in her tension, because the releases stimulated memories and their concomitant emotions. This student had already spent many years in hypnotherapy struggling to recover memories of childhood abuse. Addressing the habitual protective tensions marked a turning point in her recovery, as she then began to remember whole sequences, rather than just fragmented images, for the first time.

We are all familiar with the way in which the facial muscles can become set in a scowl of pain and bitterness. But it is not just our faces which reflect who we are and what we have experienced. Self-expression is a fact of our whole physical being.

We generally harden the musculature as we brace ourselves to face life and its future knocks; we tighten ourselves in an effort to ward off the pain itself, preventing ourselves from feeling our grief...or anything else. We set our shoulders, lower our heads, draw in our chests and screw ourselves downward in a courageous attempt to keep going. We each make individual adjustments, consistent with our own personality and habitual patterns.

I have learned to recognize grief's style. Each time I put my hands on a grieving person, I become acutely aware of how deeply our beings are imprinted with the grief experience. My ears hear ordinary conversation, but from long-contracted muscles and irritable fascia, my hands receive distress signals, almost as though the cells emit a mournful cry.

I began working with grief when I was young and recently qualified as an Alexander teacher, at a time when I was somewhat innocent of the magnitude of my student's experience. She was a young widow with three teenage children and she had been diagnosed with breast cancer. All through her chemotherapy she came to see me three times per week. She said the lessons helped tremendously with the nausea and no matter how bad she felt, she never missed an appointment. Looking back, I can see dimensions that I did not perceive at that time, dimensions with which I work much more consciously now.

The Alexander Technique is, at one level, a powerful method of touch, able to ease tensions and bring comfort with an almost miraculous immediacy. It gives the student a heightened awareness of self, an awareness that enables the student to see choices and possibilities otherwise hidden. It facilitates constructive control over one's self and, consequently, one's life. To my student, faced with a dubious prognosis, the rigors of cancer treatment, the responsibility of three children, and the loneliness of widowhood this was more significant than I realized at the time.

She asked me to give lessons to her fourteen-year old daughter as well. The daughter was clearly very tense—A shortened neck, kyphotic shoulders and general tightening bore testimony to her own inner battle. As her muscles eased, so did her fears.

Soon after that I was approached with a much more focused appeal. A mother and son wanted lessons to help them through the stages of dying; the 21 year old son had cancer. Together they wanted to live through the last months of Russell's life in the most conscious way possible, extracting the full meaning of his life and death, growing in body, mind and spirit to the last moment.

I found the request somewhat formidable, but overriding that, I felt honored to be invited to share and contribute in these last precious weeks.

Russell had already accepted his imminent death and had chosen to forego a second round of chemotherapy. What was my contribution here? Why should someone who is dying want to have Alexander lessons? What good is improved use to such a person? I still don't know how well I can answer those questions, but unquestionably the lessons were helpful to Russell in his dying process, despite the heavy medication—and helpful to his mother, Andrea, in her brave quest to accompany him every step of his final way.

On the more superficial levels, the lessons helped them to deal with their stress, releasing muscular tension. They needed all the support they could get and the lessons provided a quiet time of care and input. They both benefited in terms of increased energy after the lessons, and Russell's quality of life and sense of well-being were improved by the lessons, the same as any student's. But, above all, their desire for consciousness and mindfulness, the driving reason for having lessons, could be met by the Alexander Technique in a unique and special way, by helping to integrate mind and body tangibly, and hopefully spirit too.

I worked with Russell for the last time two days before he died. He was too weak to come to me and so Andrea asked me to come to their house. He was heavily drugged with morphine, imbuing the lesson with a very different tone. As I worked, I could feel him drift in and out of consciousness and I marveled at the special gift the Technique endows upon us, that we can become one with the person on whom we place our hands.

After that lesson Russell said he felt much better. We both knew we would not be seeing each other again.

Andrea continued to work with me after Russell's death. As a psychotherapist she specialized in working with the dying and bereaved, and because of her own and Russell's experience, she referred many people to me.

At that time it was hard for me to articulate exactly how the Alexander Technique was helpful to people in such need. I had observed that under stress, poor habits were exaggerated. Additionally, new unconscious patterns, associated with the trauma, would appear. This combination of old and new patterns increasingly interfered with functioning at a time when improved skills were most required. The Alexander Technique could reverse this trend, helping them to recontact themselves constructively .

Lacking a more comprehensive theoretical explanation, I continued to teach anyone who wanted lessons, because at the most practical level, the Alexander Technique makes people feel better!

After many years of working with grieving students, encouraging them to release sometimes long-held patterns of tension, architectured to minimize their sense of pain, I had the unfortunate opportunity to experience grief myself. My brother, and only sibling, died suddenly and shockingly, the victim of a violent murder. This personal experience gave me in-depth knowledge and understanding of the many levels at which the Alexander Technique can affect the grief experience.

It is impossible to say how I would have reacted without the influence of the Alexander Technique, so I cannot make this kind of comparison. What I did notice, though, was a strong contrast between how I thought I would react and how I did, as well as an even bigger discrepancy between what others expected me to say and feel and what I actually experienced. These differences I do attribute mostly to my training and work in the Alexander Technique.

When such a dramatic event takes place, one is pushed into a different state of consciousness, a parallel reality. Potentially, this puts one seriously out of step with day to day life. Emotional and hormonal responses come from a deep and primitive part of ourselves, and our driving instinct is to withdraw from the world. The Alexander Technique teaches us that in civilized living, instinctual response is not necessarily the most helpful. It also teaches us how to use our reason to select more facilitative behavior.

As a self-employed mother of two young children, a "run and hide" reaction would have been disastrous. On the very same morning of my brother's death I had to start choosing how to be—to put everything on hold, or to continue functioning. I chose the latter and it was immediately empowering. I found that I could still think, plan, organize, eat, laugh and socialize. I discovered that life goes on.

The Alexander Technique helped me to contain my psychological responses. Naturally enough, my first reaction was shock and also anger—anger towards my brother for knowingly putting himself at risk. What was unusual, though, was that I did not go into denial.

Faced with the incontrovertible reality of death, the general human tendency is to resort to denial. Outwardly, one acknowledges that the loved one is dead, but inside one does not quite believe that they are gone. Subtly, one continues to hope that the verdict of dead will be reversed. One expects the person to walk through the door at any moment, exactly the way one always remembered them, saying: "It was all a mistake."

The clues are not easily detected, by either oneself or the empathic listener. I remember being confused by my mother's plans to expand my brother's business after he died. After listening to her a few times I finally realized that as brave and realistic as she had been, what was in operation was a sophisticated level of denial. As gently as I could, I told her that expanding his business would be just one huge headache for her. I pointed out that he wasn't coming back to take his rightful place, and he wasn't going to say, "Thank you, you did a great job while I was away." With that, the elaborate plans dissolved and she was able to proceed with selling the business.

Denial is a form of not being in the present. It is a coping mechanism, designed to defend us against knowledge which the system construes to be too threatening, too painful, too overwhelming to survive. By removing us from reality, it simultaneously protects and hinders us.

The Alexander Technique enhanced my ability to stay in the present, to be mindful, to experience what was happening, as it was happening. This proved to be a precious gift. Denial conflicts with truth and therefore requires vigilance to maintain. It absorbs much emotional energy. By not going into denial, I was able to move directly towards acceptance. Acceptance saved me from diverting my emotions. My energies could be channeled constructively.

The experience gave me profound insight into the nature of our functioning and I was able to develop a new understanding of tension. As Alexander teachers we focus on habitual patterns of tension. I was able to distinguish two new categories: understandable tension and appropriate tension. Whereas habitual tension patterns do not serve us, interfere with our functioning and are generally historically based, understandable tension and appropriate tension are stimulated by present circumstances which are stressful. Understandable tension can be usefully inhibited to allow better functioning, but appropriate tension actually enhances functioning, being the correct response to the situation.

Yvonne, my colleague and friend, offered to give me a lesson. Although I felt very tense, I found that I did not want to let go yet. I wanted to experience my psychophysical state. It seemed such an integral part of my grief and mourning. It seemed appropriate, right, even comfortable. On reflection, it is obvious—startle pattern was the valid response to the circumstances!

In that, I also learned how important it is not to impose our sense of improvement on others. Yvonne was so gentle in her offer. I was able to say, "No," when I wanted and take her up on the offer when I was ready. She really understood my need to be left alone. Later, when she did work with me, the easing of tension also felt right, comfortable and appropriate.

Although I worked full days, spent time with my children, continued to live my life in all its detail, I was careful to spend several time periods each day on my own, doing nothing other than processing my emotions. I would sit on the steps of our house and think about my brother, what had happened, how I felt. I would cry and cry. This mourning continued intensely for the whole of the first year after he died. The second year was less sharp, but I still grieved every day. The third year, I would find myself thinking of him and crying, on a daily basis, but the grip was much lighter. Now, I think of him every day, but I am just as likely to laugh as to cry, as I remember wonderful, exciting and outrageous things about him.

I think I was able to do this because I did not fear my feelings. I knew that they could not overwhelm me, they are only a part of me, produced by me and there to be experienced and released. Feelings have power over us only when we invest our energies in keeping them at arm's length, splitting them away from their rightful position. Otherwise, they are a rich and integral dimension of ourselves.

Despite my careful and conscious work with myself, I did develop a psychosomatic symptom, which I attributed to my brother's death. About three months after he died, my knees became extremely painful and inflexible. If I had been standing, I found it difficult to bend them; if I had been sitting, I found it difficult to straighten them. The pain was general to my whole knee and equal in both. This was a mysterious malady which defied diagnosis. In some ways I was anxious about my teaching career, but deep inside I knew that this was one of the ways that I was expressing my pain and shock—I have always been prone to psychosomatic modes of expression, so this should have been no surprise.

My knees were intensely painful for about six weeks and otherwise troublesome for about two years. I could monitor my stress levels accurately by the degree of discomfort in my knees. On one occasion, within half an hour of hearing stressful news, my knees began to ache viciously.

As the years passed, my knees relented. I even found a

reference in a medical journal describing the occurrence of rheumatic-like pains after grief, confirming my understanding of the problem. I took no medication for the condition. Two things could alleviate the discomfort—one was my own conscious thought processes, the other was the intelligent touch of the Alexander lessons.

It is five years now since my brother, Michael, died. And five years seems to be the amount of time it takes to adjust to this loss, to heal. Although I would rather have learned it later, his death did teach me something which cannot be learned in any other way. This has given me an understanding, and my life and work a depth and meaning, otherwise impossible to attain. But I cannot think of the past five years without also thinking about how my knowledge of the Alexander Technique moulded it into a qualitatively different process than it might have been.

The Alexander Technique seemed to influence every aspect of my grieving. I can best describe this metaphorically. I expected grief to feel like a heavy, grey blanket which would shroud my life. Instead, it felt like a many-faceted spinning ball, one aspect somber and absorbing, the others reflective. Allowing the ball to spin through my life, I experienced an ever-changing array of life's colors and images, heightened by the creative interplay of light and dark.

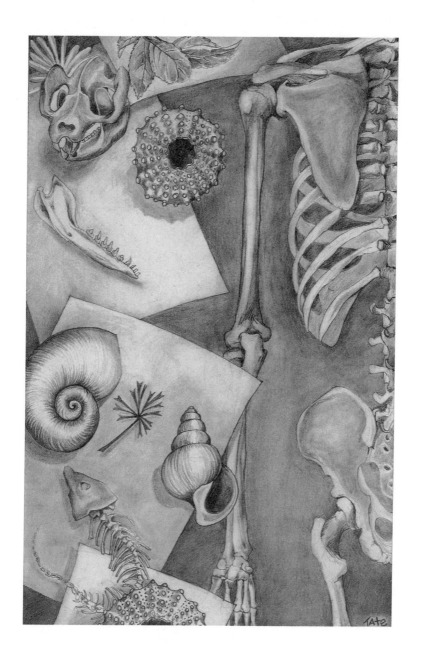

Together We Walk

& by Walton L. White

I've long been a dedicated walker although these days I don't hike much and I haven't backpacked in decades. But back in the late Sixties when I was just getting more deeply into these activities, I came across one of the first mentions I must have seen of F.M. Alexander and his work in a book titled, *The Magic of Walking*. In all honesty, that mention made no impression on me at the time, and I only know of it now from rereading the book years later.

Eventually the Alexander Technique did make a big impression on me, and I went off to London to train as a teacher. A major pleasure of that fondly remembered time were the many walks I took in that city and its surrounding countryside. Walking gave me transportation, exercise, recreation and entertainment. It still does, and more.

Over the years I've developed a deeper appreciation of the nature of walking. I've come to regard walking not as a struggle against gravity but as an alliance with it. In the effort to move, gravity becomes my accomplice, not my enemy. I see walking as less a working of muscles and more a play of balance and finesse. Walking takes the effort I must make to stand upright on two legs and gets double duty from it by using it to turn gravity's pull into locomotive energy.

Through the Alexander Technique I eventually became aware of extra effort I had been making when I walked. It taught me how much unnecessary body movement I was putting into my walk out of unconscious habit.

Before then I had lacked what most people now lack, a comparative ease of effort, whether walking across a room or a continent. For most, walking across a room won't register as a significant effort, and walking all day will bring some fatigue at the end. But when even a few steps take on a flowing ease that makes you want to take more just for the pleasure of it, you notice. When it makes your old way of walking feel labored and clunky, you notice. Whether you have exulted in the physical challenge of walking or shunned it, you are likely to take notice of this difference. That's what happened to me.

This contrast between what I call a "natural" walk with its economy of effort and motion, and the way I had been walking out of habit, (or out of attempts to follow the advice and printed instructions of various authorities, including Alexander), revealed how much extra work I had been making. The full revelation, however, didn't strike like lightning. It was a long time dawning.

As I worked with the Alexander Technique, and improved the way I used my body, movement became easier. This general sense of greater ease carried over into my walking without dramatically changing my habitual walking form. Beyond the way it teaches you to organize your body for the most beneficial condition in which to carry out any movement, the Alexander Technique doesn't limit the possible ways you may choose to move. Some ways, however, are just better than others. Some ways are basic patterns evolution worked out for us long ago; others are distortions we have imposed on these basic patterns, often with an added tax of unnecessary effort. We can become so accustomed to paying this added tax that we don't recognize it as such and take it as part of the original price.

So at first I found an improvement in whatever way I walked without automatically doing a natural walk. In fact, I discovered a number of different ways of walking that felt better than the way I had been walking before learning the Alexander Technique. It took a longer time and more experience for me to sort out the differences among them and to judge them more accurately. Mostly these differences had involved altering my arm swing this way or that, adding more hip movement here, more body lean there, lengthening my stride by this means or that, or shortening it to make my steps come faster. In general it had involved trying to coax more speed out of my walk or put more vigor into it for the sake of "exercise."

F.M. Alexander gave little direct help with these distinctions. He didn't write much about walking. In *Man's Supreme Inheritance,* however, he did lay out the basics:

"The whole physiology of walking is.... resolved into the primary movements of allowing the body to incline forward from the ankle on which the weight is supported and then preventing oneself from falling by allowing the weight to be taken in turn by the foot which has been advanced. This method, simple as it may appear, is not, however, the one usually adopted....Nearly everyone... employs physical tension in such a way that there is a tendency to shorten the spine and legs, by pressing...down through the floor instead of lightening that pressure by lengthening the body and throwing the weight forward and moving lightly and freely." (Integral Press, 1957 ed., p. 168).

There's a big difference in the effort I make walking when I merely extend my body upward over my foot and when I try to push the ground down and back away from me. In the first instance I just move my body away from the ground; in the second, in trying to push the ground away from me, I am trying to move the whole planet away from me. Since we use the ground as a frame of reference the result will read the same either way: my body moves, not the planet. It shouldn't surprise anyone, however, that it takes more effort to push the planet than to push my body.

To experience this problem, which applies not only to walking but to how we use our bodies in general, just compare pushing yourself away from something bigger, heavier or more unyielding than yourself with trying to push it away from you.

My feet exert a pressure against the ground whenever I stand on them, whether I am still or in motion. When standing still that pressure is familiarly expressed as my body weight. To apply that pressure I have to do nothing more than balance upright on two legs. In other words, in extending my body upward onto two feet, exerting my effort upward, I automatically generate all the downward pressure needed. The same is true when walking. I don't have to make a separate effort to push down against the ground to move. Yet so many of us come to do that unconsciously, out of habit.

Upward rises the path of least resistance. This seems so obvious now, but it never would have occurred to me back when I had in mind that I had to push my body forward with my muscles. If I follow this upward path correctly I can let gravity do the rest. It will pull me in the direction I want to go. Then I don't even have to push with my muscles to start my body walking forward. It takes no more effort to start that movement than to stand still.

If I want to walk forward I just give up some of the effort I've been making to stand in place by releasing my ankles and allowing them to bend. Gravity will instantly start trying to pull me off balance downward, but first it must pull me forward because my skeleton acts like a long column, the top of which will have to swing in a long arc before it will reach the ground.

If long before I have reached the point of being hopelessly off balance I have also released one hip and knee and allowed them to bend, that leg will begin to swing forward to take a step. As this begins to happen my weight automatically shifts on to the supporting leg to allow the other leg to swing free of the ground. This has all happened by reflex; I haven't had to think about making any additional, deliberate muscular effort to cause it to happen.

If I continue to let it, my foot will then swing forward and land on the ground in just the right spot to take my weight and continue the walk. Only if I were trying to land on or avoid a given spot would I deliberately have to place my foot.

The momentum my body has now gained from being pulled forward by gravity will be enough to carry my weight off my trailing leg onto my leading leg and beyond to where gravity will continue to pull my body forward into the next step and so on.

To keep my body going forward in space I must keep going upward as gravity tries to pull me downward. This doesn't mean straight up in space but upward along the angle of my body to the ground.

Even when "standing still" my body "moves." To balance upright on two feet, my postural muscles and reflexes interact to extend all the joints between the vertebrae of my spine as well as my lower limbs. These muscles and reflexes have to react to the constant subtle shifts in my center of balance from any small moves of my head and limbs and torso. Just breathing rhythmically expands and contracts the walls of my torso causing such shifts. When I walk, the joints of my hips and legs will bend, but my vertebrae must actively continue to extend my spine upward to keep all the parts suitably integrated.

The angle of my body to the ground is important here—not perpendicular, but never very far from it, just enough to let gravity continue to pull me forward. If I go up at an angle that brings my weight just over my foot as I reach my full extension upward I limit gravity's chance to help me; I will just come to a stop at the end of the step and have to start over unless I put out an extra effort with my muscles to make up for my flagging momentum.

Instead, to conserve momentum and energy I must extend my body upward at a forward leaning angle that will vary slightly according to my speed so that my weight will arrive sooner rather than later over my leading leg and gravity can begin pulling me forward before my legs are fully extended. Gravity will then help pull my supporting leg into its extension by pulling my body's weight forward off of it.

We use the muscles and bones of our bodies to overcome and direct the natural physical forces such as gravity, inertia, momentum and friction that act upon us; we turn them, where we can, to our own mechanical advantage. Getting the most mechanical advantage is what natural walking and running are all about. To push with my muscles, when I could let gravity pull, wastes effort and energy; it means using my body to resist gravity in a way that prevents it from acting to my greatest advantage. Such effort is really turned against myself and becomes self-inflicted stress.

It is easiest to become aware of this problem by exaggerating it—take giant steps. When taking the longest strides possible, walking becomes much more labored. It loses its flowing movement. It is easier, more comfortable and less tiring to take two normal strides to one giant one. Gravity helps more in the shorter stride and hinders more in the distorted, longer one.

The secret to how well we use gravity to our advantage in walking and running lies in how we stand up and balance on our legs. Walking or running is simply a matter of standing up in a new place with each step.

The importance of just standing up, and of maintaining equilibrium in walking and running, is ruefully demonstrated if you have ever seen a competitor at the end of a grueling marathon or triathlon who has pushed to the edge of total exhaustion. She is no longer capable of running, and even walking has become a supreme challenge. Her legs will still hold her up. Their large muscles still have the strength to carry her on, but the smaller postural muscles of her torso, from exhaustion and misdirection, no longer keep her spine adequately extended. She lets her torso slump down into itself or even uses other torso muscles to pull her torso down into itself as she fights to keep control of her body. In doing so she defeats herself, for unwittingly she so deranges her equilibrium that she puts herself at a terrible disadvantage against gravity and cannot control her walk and staggers about wasting her waning strength just to stay upright.

Summing up walking as the process of standing up in a new place with each step has its drawbacks as a prescription for improving walking form. Here the problem is as much psychological as physical.

If someone inexperienced in the Alexander Technique tries to carry out any description of walking form he will likely overstress, as I once did, the downward motions, pushing *down* with his feet, falling *down* onto the leg swung forward in order to stand up over it, just as in this sentence I have unnecessarily belabored the word *down.* Such downward pressure and movement happen of their own accord whether they are thought about or not, but consciously or subconsciously, he will accentuate them and pile unneeded effort onto what is going to happen anyway, creating unwanted resistance. Conscious pushing down is relatively easy to weed out. That done subconsciously, out of habit, presents the real challenge since it is not so easy to sense.

I read Alexander's words on walking long before I had experience or practical knowledge of his technique. I tried to follow his ideas and apply them to my walking and I made a mess of it. Even after I had plenty of experience and training I still couldn't apply his ideas directly to change my walk. But as my balance and my awareness of what I was doing with my body changed, I began to experience subtle changes in my walking and to understand better what was going on. I didn't "make" my body walk naturally so much as I learned how to let go of it against gravity. Like a child, I discovered my natural walk, one that had been there all the while, but unlike a child's, mine had been submerged under habits acquired in growing up.

The change happened only intermittently at first. There was no sudden enlightenment. This way of moving felt good but so did other ways of moving. Only gradually did this natural way of walking educate and inform my perception of what was happening.

I still wanted this walking to give me more of a workout, to produce more of a training effect, to raise my pulse higher, to make me sweat. In short, to conform better to the current standards of what was thought of as good exercise. There was an irony here that for a long time I couldn't see or wasn't ready to accept: I was trying to improve my walk by making more work of it.

Except when going up hills, I couldn't stir my pulse to accepted training standards no matter how fast I walked. A natural walk would just evolve smoothly into a run beyond a certain speed: only then would my pulse reach a 'training' level. I could push my walk beyond that transition speed if I distorted my stride length enough and belabored my arm swing, but that made walking so much harder that all my attention was taken up keeping the form and the pace going. It was easier and faster simply to run instead. Running took less of my attention and effort. I could enjoy my surroundings more. Even though running raised my pulse more readily it was so much more naturally efficient than a forced overstriding walk it felt like less work until I was moving far faster than the pace of that distorted walk.

I enjoyed the sweat and physicality of this type of conditioning exercise up to a point, and did as much of it as I thought I needed. Then having done my duty I would turn back to a more natural walk, which I enjoyed for itself. I always did more of the latter than the former. This wasn't out of laziness; I began taking more frequent walks. I dutifully exercised for conditioning several times a week, whereas I took walks at almost any opportunity during a day. Though this natural walk wasn't turning me into a champion athlete, it was leading me to far more exercise than my more dedicated work-out sessions.

When there were no steep hills to climb, such natural walking took little conscious effort. If I was alone, besides enjoying the easy flow of the movement and looking around at my surroundings, I sometimes thought about the naturalness of walking. This sort of walking was more natural exercise in another way; it was woven throughout the fabric of my daily doings, caught while transporting myself from here to there for whatever purpose, not isolated for its own sake in prescribed doses at times specifically appointed for exercise. Our prehistoric ancestors who first evolved as two-legged walkers didn't need to go out looking for exercise. They got all they needed looking for the next meal and staying out of harm's way.

A natural walk minimizes the effort I must make, but it doesn't eliminate it altogether. There are still times when my legs must work harder as when going uphill, climbing stairs, traveling on soft sand, or bucking a stiff head wind; each negates some of gravity's forward pull in some way. That doesn't mean I must then think about pushing down harder. That still happens automatically as I extend my body up farther and perhaps faster with each step.

There are times when the free swing of my legs is impeded, as in walking through thick, tall grass or wading through water. Anything that interferes with the natural rhythm of the leg swing will disrupt a walk and take more energy whether the interference is external like very soft or uneven terrain, or badly spaced stairs; or it is internal like trying to take too long a stride or too many stairs at once or trying to push back and down against the ground. Gravity will still be there to pull the body forward but less advantage can be taken of it.

As traveling down a steep hill can demonstrate, if I let it gravity is ready to pull my body over the ground far faster than my ability to keep my legs under me. This is just as true on level ground but rarely happens because gravity is given less chance to get my body moving in a downward direction where it can rapidly accelerate it into a free fall. But it might happen to a toddler before it masters upright equilibrium or to me if I stumble or trip over something and the delay in advancing my foot lets my body lean too far ahead of it.

Whether going downhill, on the level, or uphill, my effort should go to extend my body upward away from the ground in a manner that controls and redirects gravity to take advantage of its pull. The steeper the path, the more muscular effort I must make because my legs must bend more and lift my body weight farther with each step. As long as the line of travel isn't straight up gravity can be made to pull me forward, but beyond a certain steepness I am not walking in a natural, fully reflexive sense, but climbing with some degree of deliberation.

Stairs perhaps illustrate this more clearly. Stairs are climbed. Their spacing dictates the placement of my feet, not innate reflex. If I say I walk or run up them I mean I climb them at a walking or running pace. Because my line of travel is so much more vertical, gravity will not give me as much forward momentum, and the natural swing of the leg may not clear the height of the next step. Then I have to lift my leading leg deliberately to place my foot on the next step before extending my body up over it.

Gravity can pull more directly against this effort, so my muscles have to work harder. The task is to lift myself up onto the next step, not push down harder on the step. The less downward pressure I have to put on the leg the easier the task.

It is harder to walk up a down escalator because the foot does in effect succeed in pushing down the step instead of lifting the body, and the climber has to move faster to compensate for this loss of distance covered with each step. A similar problem arises in climbing a steep sand dune where the surface gives way under the foot. The lighter you push down the less it will give way and the easier the climb.

The trick to a natural walk is in how I let my joints bend and extend, and how and where I move a foot forward to recapture my balance and redirect my body upward—while gravity is still pulling my body forward more than it is pulling it downward. What I do with each step is in principle just what a ferryman would do to get to a point on the other side of a river: he aims for an angle upstream against the downstream pull of the river's current in such a way that the current carries him to the point he wants to reach on the other side.

I don't have to worry about propelling myself forward if I know how to lengthen myself upward correctly. The torso is not a passive passenger carried along by the legs. Nor is the head riding at the top of the spine. The way the head and torso interact with each other and the limbs determines, among other things, the center of gravity of the body, the organization of equilibrium and the way the whole body will interact with gravity. The pull of gravity upon a well-poised head will elicit postural reflexes that keep the curves of the spine tending to flatten out, gaining or maintaining the best possible functional length of the spine in any activity, even when the joints of the arms and legs are bending. Achieving this, I then can let my body walk me.

This natural way of walking builds, conserves and directs momentum, using it to carry the body over the ground from balancing on one leg onto the next with a minimum of effort in an almost imperceptibly undulating flow of movement.

For most of my life I didn't walk this way. Most people don't. When the knee that has taken the body's weight straightens it should extend the body up and slightly forward of the supporting foot. I straightened the knee too soon. Most people do. This uses up too much momentum just to carry the body upward and forward onto the front leg. Until the body gets there gravity can't pull it forward. Instead gravity will pull back on the body, taking away momentum it has previously given. Then to keep a steady pace the efforts of the legs and arms must replace lost momentum. The greater their efforts, the greater the torque generated in the body.

The extension of the rear leg acts on one side of the body to move it forward and help overcome any resistance generated by the front leg pushing back against the other side of the body. These counterforces cause a twisting action or torque around the central vertical axis of the torso. Each arm swings in the opposite direction to the leg under it. This creates a counter-torque to neutralize the torque from the leg action. So whenever the legs work harder, but especially in overstriding, they waste much of that effort in increased torque. A natural walk or run minimizes torque and arm swing.

When evolution shaped my body to walk it didn't quit there and leave me to figure out how to get all the many parts working together. Evolution also built in the best coordination of those parts for walking. I didn't have to reinvent the process or fabricate one of my own. The problem comes because evolution made me so adaptable that I can too readily and unknowingly learn to use my body in ways that hamper this innate coordination.

To improve the way I walk I have to learn where I'm interfering with that innate coordination and stop it. I have to get out of the way and let it happen. This isn't done by tinkering with parts of the walk: the foot plant or push-off, the hip, leg or arm swing. It is done by changing the way I relate to gravity with my whole being. My walk has changed not because I mastered the elements of good walking form but because I stopped attending to them. It has changed because my sense of poise and balance has changed. I have learned to give myself up to gravity not in surrender but out of respect for the mutual roles we have to play in the act of walking.

Fear of falling is a bigger impediment to natural walking than improper foot plant, stride length, arm swing, etc. These are only separate aspects of the walking process. Unconsciously fear of falling influences every aspect of the process because it relates to the sense of balance, which coordinates all the parts. If this balancing process is ever so slightly askew it can cause improper foot plant, overstriding and so forth. It can make an ordinary walker respond something like that played out marathoner struggling to keep going. In a more seemly and subtle degree without the obvious desperation he will unconsciously hold back his weight and extend his leg a little too far to brace against gravity's pull before committing his weight and balance. And out of habitual practice he will be blithely unaware that he might be doing any such thing. He will not change to a more natural coordination of his walk until his reaction to that fear changes, and he commits himself more fully and fittingly to a partnership with gravity.

The basic process that lets me stand carries in it the potential for all movement. If various parts of the standing process are turned off or on in certain patterns, I no longer stand still but walk or run or jump or squat. I don't have to take charge of each and every part of these patterns. Evolution wove these patterns and their control into the deep recesses of my being. My trying to control them by adjusting a piece of a pattern here, a piece there, will more likely disrupt or unbalance them than improve their efficiency and coordination.

I found the best way to insure their efficient functioning is to trust and respect their sovereignty. Not jump into the middle of them to try to make them heed my commands, but to get back to where they started and let them carry me from there. Learning how to lengthen my body, how to extend it upward above the ground with a minimum of effort, taught me how to walk more efficiently, more naturally, than all the direct advice I ever got on how to walk.

As my understanding of walking has evolved over time, I no longer see it as just an activity my body does on and over the surface of this planet. It is something I do along with this planet and the natural forces acting upon it. Together we walk. Without them the motions of my body would be random, futile and pointless, as would be my body's shape. This intimate sense of oneness it gives with the world and its environs perhaps explains why I, like many others, find walking so nurturing and such an antidote for so many of the stresses and strains of daily life.

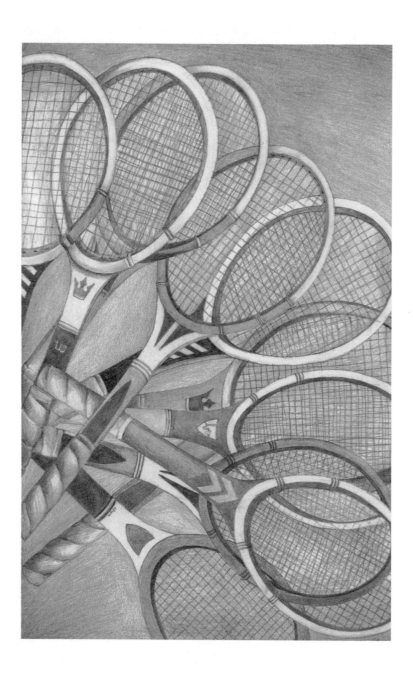

Love-40

by Barbara Kent

Teaching a physical skill is a challenge. Giving instructions is one thing, but helping someone carry out those instructions efficiently is another. As a teacher of singing I've had many opportunities to instruct a student in what to do or not to do to achieve a desired result. The bigger challenge is helping the student pay attention to the way in which the instruction is being followed. As a teacher of the Alexander Technique, I've learned a lot about paying attention and observing how instructions are carried out. This is a challenge for the teacher as well as for the student.

Recently I got to be a student again when I began taking tennis lessons. I knew tennis would be good exercise and a sport I could enjoy into my "later" years. But what was more interesting for me was the chance to apply the principles of the Alexander Technique while learning something new.

My previous experience with tennis was two group lessons as a child, and "playing at" tennis over the years. I remember being pretty awkward. With my forehand I frequently hit the ball over the fence, and my backhand seldom connected with the ball at all. It was more frustration than fun.

My first lesson this time around was great. I had no expectations. I wasn't supposed to know anything. The teacher placed the ball in the right spot and I just "directed" myself to release my neck and let my spine lengthen while I swung the racket. That allowed my body to move with ease. I felt coordinated, as if my body and limbs were working together without doing anything to make that happen. What fun. I felt more at ease than in my memory of earlier years. The game seemed easier. I was impressed; so was my teacher.

The verbal instructions in my first lesson were simple. Somehow I didn't feel as if I needed to do anything. Later I experienced the frustration of getting too much verbal instruction. I felt like I had so many things to do that I couldn't keep track of anything. I tried harder and got poorer results. I know what skill it takes to give simple instructions. As a student I really experienced the frustration of being on overload from too much instruction without enough positive experience.

In my first lesson, my teacher also relied on visual instruction by showing me the moves I was supposed to do. Having a visual picture of what was being described was very helpful. Mirroring someone's actions allowed my body to follow a physical image rather than an intellectual instruction. My whole system moved toward imitating that movement. The freer my body was from tension patterns, the better it could follow that image.

My tennis lessons showed me the value of a combination of simple verbal instruction and clear physical demonstration. The key was my level of consciousness. If my mind got too involved in telling me what to do, I tried too hard and got tied up in knots. If I just mirrored my instructor's demonstration and was not at all conscious of the way I was moving, I would fail to notice when I wasn't actually doing what I thought I was doing.

As I practiced during the year I began to experience my usual cycle of learning. The more I learned about how to play, the more invested I became, and the harder it was to be in the moment with no expectations. I had found from previous experience that as my expectations grew, my difficulties in learning grew at a commensurate pace. The stimulus to follow instructions, to do it 'right,' or to get the ball over the net got stronger as I expected more of myself. One of my goals in taking up tennis was to see if I could maintain an ability to stay in the moment, to not let the stimulus of something like a ball coming towards me interfere with my intention, or, in the words of F.M. Alexander, not to "end-gain."

End-gaining describes what happens when we become more interested in doing something than we are in *how* we are doing it. Sometimes that desire to 'do' is obvious, and sometimes more subtle or unconscious. In either case we leave the process and focus on the end. Our field of attention narrows. We are less able to know *what* we are actually doing or make any change in *how* we're doing it. By making a conscious decision to focus on the process, letting the end take care of itself, we expand our field of attention. We have the potential both to recognize and release habitual tension patterns and to pay attention to how we're executing the stroke. Non-end-gaining allows us to be conscious of *what* we're doing and *how* we're doing it *while* we're doing it. We develop the ability to think in activity.

Exploring this increased awareness makes for a very rich learning experience. It doesn't, however, suddenly free us from the pull to end-gain. That desire is a powerful undercurrent in all learning. For example, in my tennis lessons, my instructor kept saying "Follow through! You're not following through!" I heard this over and again. I knew from other sports that the follow through was essential. I had seen the follow through demonstrated, and often practiced it without the ball. I had the idea of what I was supposed to do. However, when I attempted to do what I knew I was supposed to do the ball landed way out of the court. I knew this was just a stage in learning. As a teacher I frequently tell my students to risk being wrong, knowing that trying to get it right often causes counterproductive tensions. As the student I needed to let it happen, keep a clear intention to follow through, and trust the process.

That sense of trust was not what was happening. I began to recognize a subtle resistance as the ball came. My mind got a little unclear on the form, and I experienced a moment of mental confusion. My instincts were telling me to do something else. I wasn't sure what, but that 'something else' often got the ball in the court. It felt 'right.' The urge to get the ball into the court was stronger than my intention to follow through. I was having a typical end-gaining experience.

With the help of my teacher, who asked me to notice where my racket was at the completion of my stroke, I became more conscious of what I was doing. I saw that as I swung the racket my wrist would twist and my racket would stop shortly after I hit the ball. I was also aware that I was tightening my neck and shoulders, and compressing rather than extending through my arm to finish the stroke. These were familiar mis-use patterns in my body, but I still wasn't clear about why it felt so 'right' to hit the ball that way. It reminded me of Alexander saying, "everyone wants to be right, but no one stops to consider if his idea of right is right." Finally I traced the strong impulse to hit the ball and twist my wrist in the way that 'felt right' to a carry-over from table tennis. The instincts that made me a good table tennis player had won me my Jr. High School Championship. Those muscle memories were still at work. That stroke had gotten results. The stimulus to get the ball in the court had triggered an unconscious habit established over 40 years ago!

Following the urge to do it right and get the ball in the court had led me into a strong habitual response. Being able to pay attention to what I was doing, little by little, expanded my awareness and gave me a chance to change that. Once again I needed to apply the principles of non end-gaining. In giving myself consent to not end-gain, I could 'direct' a release of my excessive neck and shoulder tension. I could focus on the stroke and not worry about the ball getting into the court. Although as a teacher I truly trust that process, I was experiencing the student's challenge of acting on it under a strong stimulus. F. M. Alexander assured us, "If you will pay attention to the means, the end will take care of itself." I knew that principle to be true, but it was interesting to see how hard it was to trust it.

Learning does not take place in a linear manner. I was to go through this cycle many times in my practice and lessons over the year. What seemed fluid and reliable one week suddenly felt awkward and foreign the next. At times the cycle was frustrating. I feared I just wasn't getting any better. The teacher in me would have reminded me that I was in a learning spiral. Being willing to stay in that process was the progress. In retrospect, the spiral is like looking through a kaleidoscope and seeing waves of clarity and integration one moment, and waves of muddled disorganization the next.

For most of us, learning has been about performing well, doing it right, and getting it quickly. That kind of focus narrows our field of attention. Being open to the risk of not 'getting it' shifts the focus and heightens our potential for an expanded field of attention. The more I'm conscious of what I'm doing, the better chance I have of doing it well. My tennis skills improved in direct relation to my willingness to risk not being 'right.' I was able to begin to find out if my idea of right was right.

Beyond Words

by Walter Carrington

When I first read Alexander's book, *Man's Supreme Inheritance*, I thought I knew how to read. I was young and sufficiently self-confident to believe that I could extract from any book the essential argument and conclusion, that I could sift facts from hypotheses, and that I could evaluate any hypotheses that were presented as being the product of the author's prejudices, preconceptions, or emotional biases. Thus, I thought I could judge a book's worth or worthlessness and the value of any contribution that it might make towards understanding and enlightenment.

Alexander's book puzzled me. I was not able to understand it, nor could I analyze it successfully; yet I could not put it aside. It was only after I met him, and first felt his hands on me, that I began to realize that here was something most unusual, something quite unique.

There is an old Chinese saying: "He who tastes, *knows.*" I think that ever since Alexander first started teaching, those who came to him experienced this. At first it was something difficult to evaluate, a feeling of lightness, a feeling of easement, and a release from constriction. But when this was followed by an evident improvement in breathing, in vocal performance, in skilled movement, in balance and poise, and in other aspects of general functioning, the results were indisputable.

He spoke of the *use of the self*, but everybody wanted an explanation of how these results were obtained. They wanted to understand the underlying mechanism, the anatomical and physiological reasons that these changes took place. But even with all the advances of modern science this information is not easy to procure. Such explanations as are available are somewhat tentative and based on a rather limited knowledge of the workings of the brain and the nervous system. When Alexander first started to teach in 1894 this area of research was in its infancy.

What he had done was to evolve a practical *technique* for effecting changes, first of all in his own behavior, and then in the behavior of others—changes that were clearly desirable because they led to tangible results. As he gained in experience, so his results consistently improved. Like everybody else he was fascinated by such scientific explanations as were forthcoming, but these only served to confirm what he already knew and what he already had established in a practical way. The nature of his *technique,* with the conscious thought processes that it involves and the quality of conscious observation and awareness from which they derive, was unaffected by any factual information that became available from other sources.

The processes that he advocated, of *conscious inhibition* and *conscious direction,* constituted an unique method of rectifying the consequences of habitual, and largely subconscious, interference with the natural functioning of the self. *Conscious inhibition* was a matter of taking a decision to withhold consent to an action in circumstances where an habitual response would otherwise follow automatically. *Conscious direction* was taking a decision that a certain movement should occur: and since the force of gravity perpetually operates in a downward direction, the primary movement required is a counteractive force in an upwards direction. Alexander observed in himself and in others that this process is commonly interfered with in most of our activities in life.

Thus a *conscious upwards direction* is needed constantly as a preventive measure. But in view of the nature of the mechanism of postural balance, this direction needs to be more specific than the word "up" would indicate, it needs to be a direction that secures the free poise of the head on the end of the spine, so that it is neither tilted backwards nor downwards. It is something that must be demonstrated, that cannot adequately be described in words.

To give a practical example of the application of this Technique: If we consider the almost universal habit of "holding the breath" in circumstances of anxiety or deep thought, this can be inhibited if there is awareness and resolution. Similarly, the impulse to "take a breath" by sniffing or gasping can be resisted if the natural process of respiration is properly understood. The intake of breath is assured by the existence of atmospheric pressure, provided that any degree of vacuum exists in the lungs. But if the whole of the rib-cage habitually collapses with each expiration, no such vacuum can exist. By means of conscious upwards direction, and the wish to employ the full natural stature of the body, the process of exhalation naturally results in the creation of a partial vacuum in the thoracic cavity: Thus the intake of breath follows automatically, and "sniffing" and "gasping" are obviated.

Alexander was not given to theoretical or philosophical speculation. He was concerned with practical procedures and results in terms of better use of our psycho-physical resources and improved functioning of the organism as a whole. If what he found by experience suggested philosophical implications, so far as he was concerned these could be left to others to explore.

Thus the Technique is something to practice and to put into practice, something that must be experienced to be understood. It cannot be learned from a book. Words, although an inevitable component in the process of communication, are woefully inadequate when it comes to the description of practical procedures. Alexander himself was acutely aware of this and was always seeking new ways of describing what he had experienced. His writings were always painstakingly achieved, and as the product of ever-growing experience, they will repay reading and re-reading by all who aspire to follow the same path.

The question is often debated as to whether his work can be regarded as truly "scientific." Professor Dart, the great anthropologist and teacher of Anatomy, looked into its anatomical and physiological background in some detail. He also practiced the Technique himself. He concluded that there is no need for further proof: As he used to say, it has proved itself; our task now should be to learn more and teach better.

However, there will always be those who crave what they call "scientific proof." They must recognize that science is largely an inductive process, one of reasoning from the particular to the general, a matter of measurement and, when possible, of statistical assessment. It is indeed a great and sure path to knowledge. But, as Alexander never tired of pointing out, his Technique is a matter for the *individual:* And whereas the simple processes of the Technique, primarily conscious thought processes, are universally applicable, their outcome or results will be as various as the individuality of the individuals concerned, difficult to quantify or to present statistically.

We all have our own individual lives to live, with our own individual experiences, our own unique perceptions and understanding of ourselves and of the world around us. But what we can all experience, by following the path that Alexander pioneered and signposted, is a taste of what he described as, "man's supreme inheritance," a realization of the full potential of our individual conscious selves.

Biographies

EDWARD AVAK was born in 1937. After finishing his academic studies in Classics and Chinese, he taught high school mathematics before being trained to teach the Alexander Technique by the Carringtons in London. He and his wife, Linda Avak, spent 1970-72 teaching the Technique in Rome and Paris. Since 1972 they have directed the Center for the Alexander Technique in Menlo Park, California, which became a teacher training course in 1982.

ANNE BLUETHENTHAL is founder and artistic director of *Anne Bluethenthal and Dancers*, a company she established in 1984 in San Francisco. She is originally from North Carolina, holds a B.A. in Dance from Oberlin College, and is certified by the North American and London Societies for Teachers of the Alexander Technique (NASTAT, STAT). Anne has performed her own and other's work throughout the U.S. She performs locally as a guest artist with various dance and theater ensembles, has been an artistic consultant and director for many Bay Area choreographers, and travels as a solo artist and teacher. As well as her work as a choreographer and performer, she has developed an innovative approach to teaching dance and training dancers. Anne has had a private practice in the F.M. Alexander Technique since 1985, and teaches dance at the ODC Performance Gallery and throughout the San Francisco Bay Area.

DEBORAH CAPLAN received her certification as a teacher of the Alexander Technique in 1953 from Alma Frank. She took lessons with F.M. Alexander, and is a founding member of The American Center for the Alexander Technique, Inc., where she is a senior faculty member of the Teacher Certification Program. Deborah studied modern dance and performed with the Pearl Primus and Jean Ardman Dance Companies. In 1956 she received her M.A. in physical therapy, and was affiliated with New York University Medical Center for eight years. She has written numerous articles on the Alexander Technique, and lectures extensively to physical therapists. She is the author of *Back Trouble: A New Approach To Prevention and Recovery Based on the Alexander Technique*. Deborah specializes in teaching the Alexander Technique to people with back problems.

WALTER CARRINGTON was born in 1915, the only child of the Rev. W.M. and Hannah Carrington. He was educated in the Choir School of All Saints, Margaret St, London, and St. Paul's School. He first had lessons with Mr. Alexander in 1935 and joined his Training Course in 1936, qualifying as a teacher of the Technique in 1939. From 1941 to 1946 he served as a pilot in the Royal Air Force, after which he returned to work as an Assistant Teacher; and then carried on the Training Course after Mr. Alexander's death in 1955. He and his wife Dilys are Directors of the Constructive Teaching Centre Ltd in London and he is a past Chairman of the Society of Teachers of the Alexander Technique (S.T.A.T.).

BARRY W. COLLINS grew up in Sydney, Australia where he went to University, receiving his degree in Dental Surgery in 1965. He trained to become an Alexander teacher under Don Burton and Elizabeth Atkinson at the Alexander Teaching Associates from 1981-1984. He lives in London and maintains an Alexander teaching practice in North London. In addition, he practices general dentistry two days a week. For the last 25 years, his main transport around London has been his bicycle, and holidays were cycling holidays. He shares his adventures with his wife, one cat, three bikes, two windsurfers, and four guitars—not simultaneously!

GALEN CRANZ went to Reed College for her B.A., and continued on to the University of Chicago for her graduate work, getting a Ph.D. in Sociology in 1971. She trained to become an Alexander teacher with Thomas Lemens from 1987-1990 in New York City. Presently she lives and teaches the Technique in Oakland, California. She also teaches at the University of California, Berkeley, in the Architecture department. She has been interested in the problem of making people comfortable since she began to analyze her own difficulties with chair design. Currently, she serves on the Board of Directors of Moving on Center, the School for Participatory Arts and Research in Oakland that integrates art and healing.

ROBERTSON DAVIES had three successive careers: first as an actor with the Old Vic Company in England; then as publisher of the Peterborough, Ontario, *Examiner,* and most recently as a university professor and first Master of Massey College at the University of Toronto, from which he retired in 1981. He has more than thirty books to his credit, among them several volumes of plays, as well as collections of essays, speeches, and *belles lettres.* As a novelist he has gained fame especially for his Deptford Trilogy—*Fifth Business, The Manticore,* and *World of Wonders*; for the Salterton Trilogy—*Tempest-Tost, Leaves of Malice,* and *A Mixture of Frailties*; for the Cornish Trilogy—*The Rebel Angels, What's Bred in the Bone,* and *The Lyre of Orpheus;* and *Murther & Walking Spirits* and *The Cunning Man.* He was the first Canadian to become an honorary member of the American Academy and Institute of Arts and Letters. He was a Companion of the Order of Canada and Honorary Fellow of Balliol College, Oxford, and he received honorary degrees from Oxford, Trinity college Dublin, the University of Wales, and McGill University, as well as from 21 other Canadian and U.S. universities. He died on December 2, 1995.

MARY HOLLAND was educated at Northfield School, Watford, England. She pursued her Arts training at Watford School of

Art, and followed her dream of acting at the Webber-Douglas School of Dramatic Art, London. She trained to become an Alexander Technique teacher at the Constructive Teaching Centre with Walter and Dilys Carrington from 1968-1970. Since 1984, she has had a private practice as an Alexander teacher in Munich, Germany, and two years later began a small training course. She has worked as a graphic designer as well as an actress. She still very much believes that the most wonderful things happen when you least expect them.

BARBARA KENT is the Director of the Teacher Certification Program at the American Center for the Alexander Technique in New York City. She was certified by the American Center for the Alexander Technique in New York City (ACAT-NY) in 1971, and has been involved in training teachers there for over 20 years.

Barbara came to the Alexander Technique through singing. She has her B.A. in music from San Jose State University in her native state of California, and her M.A. in music from Brooklyn College of the City University of N.Y.. She studied singing at the Juilliard School of Music, and sang professionally for a number of years. Ms. Kent taught music in the New York City Public Schools, at Bennett College, and at Brooklyn College of the City University. She continues to sing and to teach voice.

Barbara has taught group classes and workshops in the Alexander Technique here and abroad. She is on the Board of Directors of ACAT-NY, and was an active supporter in the early development of the national Alexander teacher's society, NASTAT.

In addition to training teachers, Ms. Kent maintains a private practice in New York City, working extensively with performers and Alexander Teachers. She continues to work on her tennis game whenever time allows.

ILANA MACHOVER is a qualified teacher of the Alexander Technique and of Medau Rhythmic Movement, and an Advanced Teacher for

Britain's National Childbirth Trust. She assists at Misha Magidov's training school for Alexander Technique teachers in London.

As part of her private practice, she runs special Eutokia courses for pregnant women. She has also conducted many workshops for midwives, childbirth educators and Alexander Technique teachers on the relevance of the Technique to childbirth.

Since 1984, she has published a number of articles on the subject, including "The Alexander way to Eutokia," in *Direction* Magazine, vol. 1, #6 (1990). Together with Angela and Jonathan Drake, she wrote *The Alexander Technique Birth Book*, published in 1993 (Robinson, UK and Stirling, US) and reissued in 1995 as *Pregnancy and Birth the Alexander Way*.

She has two children and four grandchildren.

RON MURDOCK was born and raised in Nova Scotia, Canada. He holds a Bachelor of Arts degree and Associateship in Music Diploma from Mount Allison University in New Brunswick. From 1962 to 1966 he studied privately with Professor Bernard Diamant in Montreal with scholarships from The Nova Scotia Talent Trust. Between 1966 and 1969 he completed his vocal studies with Professor Frederick Husler and Yvonne Rodd-Marling in Switzerland with scholarships from The Nova Scotia Talent Trust and The Arts Council of Great Britain.

In 1969 he moved to London, England where he established a career as a solo tenor, singing with English Opera Group and performing in oratorio performances in many English cathedrals. He gave frequent solo Lieder recitals at the Wigmore Hall and Purcell Room, London, and recorded regularly for BBC Radio 3.

Between 1976 and 1979 he trained as an Alexander Teacher with Walter and Dilys Carrington.

He has given voice/Alexander voice workshops in every major European city as well as in New York and Montreal and maintains a practice in London and Amsterdam. He has been a guest teacher at Alexander Training Schools in England, Denmark and Holland.

He now lives in Amsterdam with his American wife Sharon (a horn player in the Concertgebouw Orchestra), their baby Esther, and her daughter Nicole. Ron is the proud father of a son, Andrew, who attends a Rudolph Steiner College of Further Education in Yorkshire, England.

ALEXANDER MURRAY attended the Royal College of Music, London, and the Paris Conservatoire. He played flute in the Royal Air Force Band, and was for many years principal at the Royal Opera and the London Symphony. He studied the Alexander Technique privately with Charles Neil from 1955-1958, and trained with Walter Carrington at the Constructive Teaching Centre from 1958-1966. He has been a professor at Michigan State University, the Royal Dutch Conservatoire, and, for the past 19 years, at the University of Illinois, Urbana, Illinois. He has taught for 20 years at the National Music Camp, Interlochen. He met his wife Joan—formerly a dancer, now an Alexander teacher—while playing at the Royal Opera.

His interest and curiosity are stimulated and maintained by weekly musical evenings playing music from the Renaissance and Baroque on period instruments. His companions are a nuclear physicist, a civil engineer and a computer executive (playing traverso, harpsichord and viola da gamba respectively).

PHYLLIS G. RICHMOND received her B.A. from Barnard College, M.A. from Columbia University, and certification as an Alexander Technique teacher from John Nicholls at the Brighton Alexander Training Centre in England. She is also a Certified Laban Movement Analyst and specialist in Historical Dance. Ms. Richmond has worked with theatre, dance, and opera as performer, teacher, movement coach, director, and choreographer for over 20 years. She has published on the Alexander Technique, dance, and theatre in the US and abroad. She is presently on the faculty of the Meadows School of the Arts at Southern Methodist

University in Dallas, TX and the Blair School of Music at Vanderbilt University in Nashville, TN.

VIVIEN SCHAPERA was born in 1956 in Cape Town, South Africa. She was trained in the Alexander Technique by Joyce Roberts in South Africa and Walter Carrington in London, and was certified as a teacher in 1983 by Walter Carrington. She received her Masters in Psychology from the University of Cape Town in December 1984. She and her family immigrated to the United States in October, 1991, and started a training course in September 1993. Along with her interest in the Technique, Vivien pursues a wide range of other interests including: psychology, martial arts, cooking, metaphysics, healing, and writing. She recently wrote and published, *How to Establish and Maintain a Strong Client-Base: A Guide to Alexander Teachers* in 1995. She has been married to her husband Neil for 15 years, and has two sons, Aidan, nine, and Jason, six.

JERRY SONTAG is the publisher and editor of Mornum Time Press, a family-run business founded in 1993. In 1994, Jerry edited and published *Thinking Aloud: Talks on Teaching the Alexander Technique* by Walter Carrington. A second volume of Mr. Carrington's talks is planned.

Jerry trained to become an Alexander teacher at the Center for the Alexander Technique in Menlo Park, California. He has maintained a private teaching practice in San Francisco since 1985, and served as Chairman of the North American Society of Teachers of the Alexander Technique (NASTAT) in 1991. He lives in San Francisco with his wife Lorelei and their son Samuel.

WALTON LAURENCE WHITE, known as Larry, is a native of Los Angeles. He completed his B.A. at UCLA in Theatre Arts in 1963, and spent several years in the graduate film program. Larry did his teacher training in London from 1973-1976 with Patrick Macdonald.

Larry has lived and taught the Technique in Santa Monica, California since 1976. "Living in a locale that has an ocean, beaches, deep canyons right in the neighborhood and mountains not far off, I can be found most mornings after first light letting my body walk me around north Santa Monica, enjoying the walking, the walkers and the spectacle."

SELECTED BILBIOGRAPHY

Alexander, Frederick Matthias. *Articles and Letters* (Notes and Foreword by Jean M.O Fischer). London: Mouritz (STAT Books), *1995*.

———— *Constructive Conscious Control of the Individual*. London: Methuen, *1932*.

———— *Man's Supreme Inheritance*. New York & London: E. P. Dutton & Co., *1918*. (An annotated edition is available from Mouritz, London.)

———— *The Universal Constant in Living*. New York: E.P. Dutton & Co., *1941*.

———— *The Use of the Self*. London: Integral Press, *1946*.

Barlow, Wilfred. *The Alexander Technique*. New York: Alfred A. Knopf, *1979*.

Carrington, Walter. *Thinking Aloud: Talks on Teaching the Alexander Technique*. San Francisco: Mornum Time Press, *1994*.

Carrington, Walter & Seán Carey. *Explaining the Alexander Technique: The Writings of F. Matthias Alexander*. London: Sheildrake Press, *1992*.

———— *Walter Carrington on the Alexander Technique: In Discussion with Seán Carey*. London: Sheildrake Press, *1986*.

Davies, Robertson. *The Cunning Man*. New York: Viking, *1995*

———— *The Deptford Trilogy*. Harmonswordth, Middlesex, England: Penguin Books, *1987*.

———— *The Lyre of Orpheus*. New York: Viking, *1989*.

———— *Murther & Walking Spirits*. New York: Viking, *1991*.

———— *The Rebel Angels*. New York: viking, *1982*.

———— *A Voice from the Attic*. rev. ed. New York: Penguin, *1990*.

———— *What's Bred in the Bone*, New York: Viking: *1985*.

Gelb, Michael. *Body Learning*. 2nd edition. New York: Henry Holt & Co, *1994*.

Nicholls, John. *The Alexander Technique in Conversation with John Nicholls & Seán Carey*. London: Nicholls & Carey, *1991*.

Pinsky, Mark A. *The Carpal Tunnel Syndrome*. New York: Warner Books, *1993*.

Westfeldt, Lulie. *F. Matthias Alexander: The Man and his Work*. Long Beach, California: Centerline Press, *1986*.

The Chair

Bronson, Po. *Bombardiers*. New York: Random House, *1995*.

Cranz, Galen. *The Chair: Rethinking Body, Culture and Design*. New York: W.W. Norton, forthcoming *1998*.

———— *The Politics of Park Design: A History of Urban Parks in America*. Cambridge, Massachusetts: M.I.T. Press, *1982*.

Gideon, Sigried. *Mechanization Takes Command*. New York: Oxford University Press, *1948*.

Johnson, Don. *Body: Recovering Our Sensual Wisdom*. Berkeley: North Atlantic Books, *1992*.

Mandal, A.C. "The Correct Height of School Furniture." *Human Factors*, Volume *24*, Number *3*, June *1982*, p. *257-269*.

Petroski, Henry. *The Evolution of Useful Things*. New York: Knopf, *1992*.

Rittel, Horst and Webber, Melvin. "Dilemnas in a General Theory of Planning." *Policy Science*. Number 4, pp. 155-169.

Rudofsky, Bernard. *Now I Lay Me Down to Eat*. Garden City, NJ: Anchor, *1980*.

Parallel Lives

Gesell, Arnold. *The Embryology of Behavior*. New York, London: Harper, *1945*.

Groner, Rudolf, Groner, Marina, Bischof, Walter F. *Methods of Heuristics*. Hillsdale, NJ: Lawrence Erlbaum, *1983*.

Hadamard, Jacques. *The Psychology of Invention in the Mathematical Field*. New York: Dover, *1945*.

Herrick, C. Judson. *The Evolution of Human Nature*. Austin: University of Texas, *1956*.

Lorenz, Konrad. *Studies in Animal and Human Behavior*. Cambridge: Harvard University Press, *1970*.

Mead, George H.. *Mind, Self and Society*. Chicago: University of Chicago Press, *1934*.

Pais, Abraham. *Subtle is the Lord*. New York: Oxford University Press, *1982*.

Polya, George. *How to Solve It*. Princeton, NJ: Princeton University Press, *1945*.

———*Collected Papers*. Cambridge: M.I.T., *1984*.

———*Mathematical Discovery*. New York: Wiley, *1962*.

———*Mathematics and Plausible Reasoning*. Princeton: Princeton University Press, *1954*.

——— with Szego, G. *Aufgaben und Lehrsätze aus der Analysis*. Berlin: Springer, *1954*.

Floating Thoughts

Caplan, Deborah. *Back Trouble*. Gainesville, Florida: Triad Publishing Company, *1987*.

Gorman, David. *The Body Moveable*. Guelph, Ontario: Ampersand Press, *1981*.

The Actor's Consciousness

Burge, Paul. "Acting and Inhibition." The Congress Papers, Brighton: *1988*, *Direction*. Volume *1* Number *5*, *1989*, pp. *68-72*.

Diamond, Joan. "The Actor & the Neutral State." *Direction*.

Volume *1* Number *10*, *1994*, pp. *387-388*.

Gray, John. "The Alexander Technique and the Actor." *More Talk of Alexander*. Editor, Dr. Wilfred Barlow. London: Victor Gollancz, *1978*, pp. *204-211*.

Johnson-Chase, Michael. "Do We Cry Because We Grieve or Do We Grieve Because We Cry?" *Direction*. Volume *1* Number *9*, *1993*, pp. *361-364*.

Lee, Nicolette. "Stanislavsky and the Alexander Technique." *The Alexander Journal*. Number *9*, Summer *1988*, pp. *16-20*.

Levine, Richard. "Acting and the Alexander Technique." *NASTAT News*. Number *14*, Winter *1992*, pp. *10-11*.

Rodrigue, Jean-Louis. "The Meisner Method and the Alexander Technique." *NASTAT News*. Number *25*, Summer *1994*, p. *22*.

Schirle, Joan. "Preparing a Role." *NASTAT News*. Number *23*, Winter *1994*, pp. *13-14*.

Stanislavski, Constantin and Rumyantsev, Pavel. *Stanislavski on Opera*. Trans. Elizabeth Reynolds Hapgood. New York: Theatre Arts, *1975*.

Stanislavski, Constantin. *An Actor Prepares*. Trans. Elizabeth Reynolds Hapgood. New York: Theatre Arts, *1946*.

Stanislavski, Constantin. *Building a Character*. Trans. Elizabeth Reynolds Hapgood. New York: Theatre Arts, *1949*.

Stanislavski, Constantin. *Creating a Role*. Trans. Elizabeth Reynolds Hapgood. New York: Theatre Arts, *1961*.

The Alexander Technique in Childbirth

Dick-Read, Grantley. *Childbirth Without Fear*. *5*th Edition. New York: Harper & Row, *1985*.

Gaskin, Ina May. *Spiritual Midwifery*. Summertown, TN: The Book Pub. Company, *1978*.

Haire, Doris. *The Cultural Warping of Childbirth*. Hillside, NJ: International Childbirth Education Association, *1972*.

Kitzinger, Sheila. *Freedom and Choice in Childbirth*. New York:
　　Viking, *1987*.
Kitzinger, Sheila. *Pregnancy and Childbirth*. rev. ed. New York:
　　Penguin, *1989*.
Lamaze, Fernand. *Painless Childbirth*. Chicago: Henry Regnery, *1970*.
Machover, Ilana and Drake, Angela and Drake, Jonathan. *The
　　Alexander Technique Birth Book*.. London: Robinson, *1993*.
　　Reissued as *Pregnancy and Birth the Alexander Way*.
　　Robinson, 1995.
Mitford, Jessica. *The American Way of Birth*. New York: Dutton, *1992*.
Noble, Elizabeth. *Essential Exercises for the Childbearing Year*.
　　Boston: Houghton Mifflin, *1976*.
Odent, Michel. *Birth Reborn*. New York: Pantheon, *1984*.
Wagner, Marsden, *Pursuing the Birth Machine*. Camperdown NSW
　　Australia: Ace Graphics, *1994*.

Born to Sing

Alexander, Frederick Matthias. *Constructive Conscious Control of
　　the Individual*. London: Methuen, *1932*.
———— *Man's Supreme Inheritance*. New York & London: E. P.
　　Dutton & Co., *1918*. An annotated edition is available from
　　STAT Books, London.
———— *The Universal Constant in Living*. New York: E.P. Dutton
　　& Co., *1941*.
———— *The Use of the Self*. London: Integral Press, *1946*.
Carrington, Walter. *Thinking Aloud: Talks on Teaching the
　　Alexander Technique*. San Francisco: Mornum Time
　　Press, *1994*.
Chatwin, Bruce. *Songlines*. *1*st American Edition. New York:
　　Viking, *1987*.
De Bono, Edward. *The Mechanism of Mind*. New York: Simon &
　　Schuster, *1969*.
Husler, Frederick & Rodd-Marling, Yvonne. *Singing: The Physical*

Nature of the Vocal Organ. A Guide to Unlocking the Singing Voice. New York: October House, *1965.* Available through T. Rodd, *3* Briar Walk, London SW*15* 6UD. England. International money order payable to T. Rodd for UK 20 pounds (includes an accompanying cassette, post and packing).

Lowen, Alexander. *Depression and the Body.* Baltimore, MD: Penguin, *1972.*

Negus, Victor Ewings. *The Comparative Anatomy and Physiology of the Larynx.* New York: Grune & Stretton, *1949.*

Stevens, Chris. *Towards a Physiology of the Alexander Technique.* London: STAT Books, *1995.*

Veras, Raymundo. *Children of Dreams, Children of Hope.* Chicago: Henry Regnery Company, *1975.*

Watts, Alan. *The Wisdom of Insecurity.* New York: Pantheon, *1951.*

Grabbing the Bird by the Tale

Alexander, Frederick Matthias. *Articles and Letters* (Notes and Foreword by Jean M.O Fischer). London: Mouritz (STAT Books), *1995.*

———— *Man's Supreme Inheritance.* London: Mouritz, *1996 (An annotated edition by Jean Fischer)*

Clynes, Dr. Manfred. *Sentics: The Touch of the Emotions.* New York: Anchor Press/Doubleday, *1978.*

Dart, Raymond Arthur. *Skill and Poise.* (Introduction by Alexander Murray) London: STAT Books, *1996.*

Dewey, John. How We Think. *Middle Works,* Volume 6, SIU Press, *1910.*

Fethney, Michael. *The Absurd and the Brave* (Foreword by Lord Asa Briggs). Sussex, England: The Book Guild, *1990.*

Huang, Chungliang Al. *Embrace Tiger, Return to Mountain. The Essence of T'ai Chi.* Moab, Utah: Real People Press, *1973.*

———— & Jerry Lynch. *Mentoring: The Tao of Giving and*

Receiving Wisdom. New York: Harper Collins, *1995*.

James, William. *Talks to Teachers*. New York: W.W. Norton, *1958*.

Jones, Frank Pierce. *Freedom to Change (formerly Body Awareness in Action)* London: Mouritz, *1997*.

McLeod, Rosslyn. *Up From Down Under*. Canterbury, Victoria, Australia: Roslyn McLeod, *1994*.

Shawn, Ted. *Every Little Movement*. New York: Dance Horizons, *1963*. A book about Delsarte.

Grief

Kübler-Ross, Elisabeth. *On Death and Dying*. New York: Collier Books, *1969*.

Together We Walk

Alexander, Frederick Matthias. *The Use of the Self*. London: Integral Press, *1946*.

Sussman, Aaron & Goode, Ruth. *The Magic of Walking*. New York: Simon and Schuster, *1967*.

Beyond Words

Alexander, Frederick Matthias. *Articles and Letters* (Notes and Foreword by Jean M.O Fischer). London: Mouritz (STAT Books), *1995*.

——— *Man's Supreme Inheritance*. New York & London: E. P. Dutton & Co., *1918*

RESOURCES

Alexander Technique Professional Organizations

The following organizations are affiliated with each other and have similar teaching standards. They can provide you with a list of teachers in your area who have completed the required three years of training to become certified. It is often worthwhile to contact several teachers in your area before deciding upon the teacher best suited to your needs.

Australia
Australian Society of Teachers of the Alexander Technique
P.O. Box 716
Darlinghurst
NSW 2010
Tel: 008.339.571

Brazil
Brazilian Association of Alexander Technique
Rua dos Miranhas, 333
Pinheiros - 05434
Sao Paulo

Canada

Canadian Society of Teachers of the Alexander Technique
Box 47025
#12 - 555 West 12th Avenue
Vancouver, B.C. V5Z 3XO
Tel: 604.689.9102

Denmark

*Danish Society of Teachers of the Alexander Technique*Sandhojen 18
DK-2720, Vanlose
Tel: 31.741366

Germany

German Society of Teachers of the Alexander Technique
Gesellschaft der Lehrer
der F.M. Alexander Technik e V
Postfach 5312
D- 79020 Freiburg
Tel: 07.61.47.5995

Israel

Israeli Society of Teachers of the Alexander Technique
c/o Gideon Avrahami
Kibbutz Ein-Shemer
M.P. Menashe 37845
Israel
Tel: 06.374196

Netherlands

Netherlands Society of Teachers of the Alexander Technique
PO Box 15591
NL-1001 NB Amsterdam
Tel: 020.625.31.63

South Africa
South African Society of Teachers of the Alexander Technique
12 Cavalcade Road
Green Point 8001
South Africa
Tel: 021.429.3440

Switzerland
Swiss Society of Teachers of the Alexander Technique
Schweizerischer Verband der Lehrer der F.M. Alexander Technique
Postfach
CH-8032 Zurich

United Kingdom
Society of Teachers of the Alexander Technique
20 London House
266 Fulham Road
London SW 10 9EL
0171.351.0828

United States of America
North American Society of Teachers of the Alexander Technique
3010 Hennepin Avenue South, Suite 10
Minneapolis, Minnesota 55408
800.473.0620

Mail Order Book Catalogues

Besides your local library or bookstore, there are two excellent sources for books on the Alexander Technique:

STAT Books
20 London House
266 Fulham Road
London SW 10 9EL
England
0171.351.0828

NASTAT Books
3010 Hennepin Avenue South,
Suite 10
Minneapolis, Minnesota 55408
800.473.0620

About Mornum Time Press

Mornum Time Press is a family-run business founded in 1993. The press specializes in books on education, with its first three titles focusing on the F.M. Alexander Technique. The Press will be coming out with a children's book in 1998. Jerry Sontag is the publisher and editor of Mornum Time Press, as well as a teacher of the Alexander Technique.

Also available from Mornum Time Press: *Thinking Aloud: Talks on Teaching the Alexander Technique* by Walter Carrington. ISBN 0-9644352-0-9, $22.00. To order, send $22.00 + $3.00 postage to Mornum Time Press, 381 Bush Street, Suite 500, San Francisco, California 94104. A second volume of Walter Carrington's talks on the Alexander Technique will be available in 1998.